NEW WORLD REGIONALISM
LITERATURE IN THE AMERICAS

As we witness nations being torn apart by warring factions, each claiming a particular parcel of land as its native soil; as industry and environmentalists argue over the development versus the protection of ecosystems; as once-common assumptions about universal humanist values increasingly come into question, it is clear that regionalism is more than nostalgic 'local colour.' Regionalism involves the dynamic interplay of political, cultural, and psychological forces.

New World Regionalism reconsiders outdated definitions by tracing the development of regionalist fiction in North and South America since the early 1800s. Regionalism has particular implications in the New World, where isolated cultures inhabiting distinct geographic locales are doubly marginalized, first by their peripheral status vis-à-vis industrialized urban centres, and second by the legacy of European colonization.

Drawing on examples from Brazil, Mexico, the United States, and Canada, David M. Jordan shows that the underdeveloped countries of South America, the superpower United States, and the only-recently 'post-colonial' Canada have a common heritage in literary appropriations of the environment, or New World regionalism.

DAVID M. JORDAN is Instructor in the Department of Humanities and Social Sciences, Red Deer College.

THEORY/CULTURE

Editors:
Linda Hutcheon, Gary Leonard,
Janet Paterson, and Paul Perron

DAVID M. JORDAN

New World Regionalism
Literature in the Americas

UNIVERSITY OF TORONTO PRESS
Toronto Buffalo London

© University of Toronto Press Incorporated 1994
Toronto Buffalo London
Printed in Canada

ISBN 0-8020-0568-3 (cloth)
ISBN 0-8020-6989-4 (paper)

Printed on acid-free paper

Canadian Cataloguing in Publication Data

Jordan, David, 1956–
    New world regionalism : literature in the Americas

(Theory/culture)
Includes index.
ISBN 0-8020-0568-3 (bound)   ISBN 0-8020-6989-4 (pbk.)

1. Regionalism in literature. 2. South America –
Literatures – History and criticism. 3. American
literature – History and criticism. 4. Canadian
literature (English) – History and criticism.
I. Title. II. Series.

PN605.R4J67 1994   809'.9332   C94-930333-X

University of Toronto Press acknowledges the financial assistance to its
publishing program of the Canada Council and the Ontario Arts Council.

This book has been published with the help of a grant from the
Canadian Federation for the Humanities, using funds provided by the
Social Science and Humanities Research Council of Canada.

Contents

NEW WORLD REGIONALISM

Introduction

Recent approaches to regionalism have brought some provocative new ideas to an old subject. It seems increasingly clear that regionalism means more than just 'local colour'; it involves a dynamic interplay of political, social, and psychological forces, which in turn impart an aesthetic tension to textual representations of regionalism. New approaches to regionalism shed new light on old works, and also suggest new ways of looking at some more recent works that treat such topical issues as our relation to the natural environment, and the relation of marginal communities to the larger social and political worlds within which they exist.

Regionalism has particular implications in the New World, where it has never been far removed from politics. With the declarations of political independence that swept the countries of the Americas from the late eighteenth century through the nineteenth century came the desire for a corresponding aesthetic and cultural independence, and literary depictions of exotic environments seemed to be one obvious means of expressing New World difference. The history of New World regionalism is problematic, though, because prevailing perceptions of the relation between the New World and the Old have shifted over time, as have perceptions of our relation to the natural environment, and even of the relation between fiction and the world it purportedly represents. The task confronted by New World regionalists is further complicated by the shifting set of sociopolitical variables that each nation brings to the equation.

Writing in 1815, Simón Bolívar described the postcolonial condition when he explained that he and his compatriots belonged to neither New World nor Old, but inhabited 'un mundo aparte.'[1] While non-regionalist authors have occasionally chosen to explore the ideological and aesthetic implications of inhabiting this in-between world, attention focused on local environments forces regionalist authors to confront directly the conflicts between inherited Old World languages and cultures and the New World environment. The authors of *The Empire Writes Back* identify three broad phases of postcolonialism, only the most recent of which self-consciously subverts hierarchical systems that would deny the expression of difference.[2] As we shall see in the ensuing chapters, however, New World regionalists have always problematized the 'double vision' inherent in postcolonial discourse.[3]

The 'discovery' of a 'New World' meant very different things to European arrivals in the North and the South, and to this day regionalism continues to respond to cultural needs stemming from these historical differences. Colonizers were dispatched to the southern Americas for the express purpose of enriching Old World coffers: the professed intention of early colonizers such as Diego Velázquez and Hernán Cortés was to amass gold for the crown and souls for the church. (Contradictory accounts in Cortés's official correspondence and the personal memoirs of one his crew members suggest that the colonizers' true goals may have been less loyal to church and state, but no less proprietary.)[4] The South has never recovered from its original role as a source of plunder for Europe. While cosmopolitan centres such as Rio de Janeiro and Buenos Aires revel in their European contacts, the vast majority of Latin Americans suffer from poverty and underdevelopment.

In 'Backwardness and Underdevelopment,' António Cândido traces two broad phases of Latin America's cultural self-awareness, and describes regionalism's role as central to both phases. At first, poverty was widely viewed as evidence of undeveloped potential. In this phase, authors used indigenous environs to justify New World poverty by portraying regions as primitive yet abounding with potential; the result was what Cândido describes as 'compensatory idealism,' a regionalism that served up exotic images catering to European tastes. Then, with a growing awareness that poverty was not transitory, but endemic, self-awareness changed from 'underdevelopment' to a perceived 'backwardness.' In the late nineteenth century, as perceptions shifted from optimistic visions of future development to resentment of present poverty, regionalism turned from idealism to realism, offering images of rural poverty as evidence of continued exploitation.

Perhaps because of the more violent initial conquest and the continued troubled relations between descendants of the conquerors and the land they inhabit, Latin America has a much richer tradition of regionalism than the United States and Canada. The *novela de la tierra* is firmly established in south American literary studies, and the genre does not have the pejorative connotations that 'regionalism' has in English studies. Whereas the only concerted regionalist movement in North America to have gained national attention was the Fugitive/Agrarian movement in the southern United States in the 1920s and 1930s,[5] *regionalismo* movements have proliferated throughout the history of South American literature. The 1920s and 1930s were particularly productive for South American regionalism, and some of the continent's most provocative avant-garde writing emerged from its *regionalismo* movements.[6] In this study, I will discuss just one of these modernist regionalist movements, that which was based in northeastern Brazil.

Early European arrivals in North America saw their mission more as settlement than conquest, and U.S. settlers differed from their Canadian counterparts in the moral imperative they imparted to this job of settlement. The American Revolution and subsequent Declaration of Independence outlined the moral destiny of a people bent on founding a New World: early settlers viewed the virgin land as an opportunity to relinquish Europe's sins and begin again with a pure conscience. Unlike their counterparts in the southern Americas, U.S. settlers had no need to keep a running tally of 'converted savages' with which to impress sponsors when they wrote home for more money, so the continent's native inhabitants were less systematically imprisoned and enslaved; they were killed, converted, or imprisoned only when they refused to be driven off their land and into the void beyond the frontier. The land was cleared, mined, and otherwise 'cultivated,' but few seem to have noted the irony inherent in razing the unfamiliar landscape in order to found a 'new world.' The contradiction between Manifest Destiny on the one hand and the slaughter of natives and the rape of the land on the other imparts an ideological tension to early U.S. regionalism: in fiction, regions became a symbolic ground upon which forces of conquest were rationalized through mythic figures personifying the moral imperatives of Manifest Destiny.[7] As those mythic figures passed into the cultural fabric, regionalism became instrumental in the suppression of alien cultures; homesteading narratives would portray Manifest Destiny as the levelling agent overcoming ethnic disparity, and moral purity as the source of settlers' claims on the land.

Canada had a similar history, except that settlement was not propelled by the same moral imperative; Canadian confederation was more an alliance of convenience than a pact of moral responsibility. While the prevailing myth of U.S. settlement may have been that of the innocent in the garden, the prevailing myth of Canadian settlement might be that of the 'garrison mentality' described by Northrop Frye.[8] Frye's mythology may oversimplify complex conflicts between commerce and idealism, as does the American myth of innocence, but it describes an important difference between Canadian and U.S. settlement. Canadian settlers were faced not with a unified frontier and the moral imperative of pushing back the borders of barbarism, but with a porous coastline, and they were motivated more by purely practical concerns of protecting their commercial interests. Canadian settlement entailed destruction of the environment and exploitation of native inhabitants, as did settlement in the U.S., but early Canadian literature shows less evidence of a felt need to justify ideological contradictions. Early Canadian regionalism responded to different cultural needs; rather than perpetuate ideological justifications for westward expansion, it tended to portray colonial outposts as centres of civilization, and to fortify the borders of these outposts by defending the civilization within against the external threat of both harsh climate and 'savage' natives. To the present day, Canadian regionalism continues to be primarily concerned with a confrontation between human settlement and the vast terrain of an inhospitable continent, with staking a claim on the land through naming.[9]

The evolving poetics of representational fiction has offered various means of responding to the problematic task of representing regionalism. The contemporary Canadian regionalist Robert Kroetsch summarizes a century of evolving poetics: 'Most books contain the idea of world. Not all contain the idea of book. In those that contain both we get a sense of how book and world have intercourse' ('Fear of Women' 73). To this cryptic summary of realist, modernist, and postmodernist approaches to representation, I would add an earlier romantic view of fiction's referent as neither book nor world, but 'a world elsewhere' – a transcendent realm for which both nature and language are mere symbols. These shifting views of the relation between book and world would determine what constitutes a region and how a region could best be represented in the pages of narrative fiction.

The poetics of romantic fiction offered a means of portraying regions symbolically as an abstract ground upon which opposing ideological and cultural forces could be reconciled. Early New World regionalists seemed less concerned with describing New World environments than with justifying the conquest of native inhabitants and the settlement of the land. Nevertheless, regionalist literature must necessarily be grounded in real-world geography, and early nineteenth-century authors were faced with the challenge of reconciling romanticism's transcendental poetics with the attention to the details of real-world geography that is essential to regionalism. Examples from Brazil and the U.S. in chapter 1 will illustrate two different responses to this challenge of reconciling romantic ideology with New World settlement.

The rising prominence of realism in the latter decades of the nineteenth century offered New World regionalists a means of pursuing the attention to local detail that is an important part of regionalism. Realist authors, however, tended to ignore the ideological conflicts underlying New World settlement, as well as the hidden ideology of realist representation, or as Ashcroft and Tiffin describe it, 'the power of the word to make worlds' (138). Earnest attempts to record regional details proliferated in the late nineteenth century, and these pedestrian examples of local-colour realism are responsible for popular perceptions of regionalist literature that persist to the present day.

Late nineteenth-century regionalism also exhibits an affinity with naturalism, and the politics of regionalism give a distinct bent to naturalism's search for determinist laws of existence. In Brazilian literature, we will see the epitome of regionalism's complicity with realism and naturalism in Euclides da Cunha's *Os sertões*, an attempt to link regional identity to local environment that combines journalism, fiction, and science. In chapter 1 I will also look at examples of U.S. popular literature from the late nineteenth century that exhibit an emerging awareness of an inherent contradiction between realism's avowed objective disinterest and the personal attachment to a particular place that lies at the heart of regionalism.

Early twentieth-century innovations in prose poetics offered ways of reversing realism's objective gaze to examine more closely the internal workings of human perception. Examples in chapters 3 and 4 will demonstrate how authors adapted modernist poetics to regionalism by conflating epistemological and aesthetic borders with borders that define regional identity. Modernism's introspective gaze often led to a sense of alienation, and regionalism frequently politicized this alienation by portraying centralized social and political systems as threats to regional identity.

Finally, evidence of regionalism's ongoing vitality can be found in works widely recognized as examples of postmodern poetics. Carlos Fuentes uses a poetics of multiplicity to suggest that modernization has not flattened the spirit of place in modern-day Mexico City, but that the Aztec world upon which Mexico City was built survives and that it is responsible for the endless cycle of repression and rebellion that marks twentieth-century Mexican history. In his depictions of the Canadian prairie, Robert Kroetsch situates his narratives on the region's borders, and incorporates both native and European myth into a modern-day narrative that explodes any fixed ideas of region and nation.

Before proceeding with my discussion of New World regionalism, I should clarify my use of the term 'regionalism.' A popular dictionary of literary terms defines regionalism as 'the tendency of some writers to set their works in a particular locality, presented in some detail as affecting the lives and fortunes of the inhabitants' (Shipley). This interaction between a community and the natural environment it inhabits is the starting point of regionalism, but attempts to explain how this interaction between people and place might best be depicted in literature have been ambiguous at best. One critic describes the source of regional identity as a 'mysterious force ... the mystery of place' (Everson 208); another refers to the 'indefinable air' that gives a specific locale its distinctive character (Norris, 'An Opening for Novelists' 1112); yet another specifies that regionalist fiction must not only be set in a particular place, but 'derive actual substance from that location' (Stewart 370). References to such nebulous entities as a 'mysterious force,' an 'indefinable air,' or a 'substance' do little to clarify the subject of regionalist fiction.

Mary Austin – herself a prolific regionalist author – offers an alternative when she identifies regionalism's referent not as a catalogue of quantifiable entities, but as experience itself. She describes the regionalist author not merely as an observer, but as one who 'has lived deeply and experientially into his own environment' (105). Austin's suggestion that authors might examine a lived experience, rather than try to quantify external phenomena, suggests an alternative approach to an aesthetic of regionalism: if we consider this distinct regional *experience* as the subject of fiction, we might examine ways in which fiction reflects not only distinctive external facts, but also a distinct regional existence governed by local forces. Although she portrays this regional experience in her own fiction,[10] Austin's critical explanation that 'the region must enter constructively into the story, as another character, as the instigator of plot' (105) offers no alternative to the traditional techniques of local-colour realism.

Traditional definitions ignore a crucial aspect of regionalism: its marginality. Because a region is by definition a small part of a larger whole, regionalism necessarily proceeds from a de-centred world-view, and this de-centred world-view distinguishes regionalism from other place-based literature, such as nature writing or travel writing. Regionalism begins with an author's privileged access to a community that has evolved through generations of interaction with a local environment, and whose identity is defined in opposition to a larger world beyond regional borders. Exactly who has access to this regionalist perspective has always been a contentious issue. Hamlin Garland declared defiantly in 1894 that the regionalist novel (or what he referred to as 'the local novel') 'could not have been written in any other place or by any one else than a native' (*Crumbling Idols* 64). Walter Wells offers more moderate criteria when he says, 'What counts is that a writer, whatever his regional tenure, know the region intimately, and that this intimacy find its way into the aesthetic makeup of his writing' (7–8). Wells contradicts Garland's claim by referring to two American authors known for their personal attachment to particular regions: Robert Frost, born in California, and Robinson Jeffers, born in Pennsylvania (7). Although place of birth may not be the final arbiter of who can lay claim to being a regionalist 'insider,' there is no doubt that regionalism stems from a deep personal involvement with a particular place, a lived experience that is not available to the casual observer.

The term 'regionalism' has been used recently in a metaphoric sense to allude to any marginalized 'space,'[11] but unless we retain the term's literal denotation of a recognizable parcel of real-world geography, regionalism overlaps with other disciplines and the meaning of the term becomes impossibly diffuse.[12] The emerging field of 'bioregionalism' emphasizes regionalism's ties to the natural environment, and a recent outpouring of 'bioregional' criticism considers local human culture as an integral part of natural ecosystems.[13] Although 'bioregionalism' can often refer to the same back-to-nature movements that have always accompanied critiques of modernization,[14] when environmental approaches to regionalism are accompanied by an awareness of the theoretical implications of how thinking regionally can challenge prevailing assumptions about cultural homogeneity, this recent approach adds important insights to regionalism's traditional ties to geography.

In 'The Aesthetics of Regionalism,' written half a century before the recent boom in environmentalism, John Crowe Ransom described how regionalism need not be tied to anachronistic depictions of local geography, but might be capable of adapting to social and economic change. He traces the evolution of regional culture from a community's initial contact with local environs – a purely utilitarian relationship that involves extracting a subsistence from local resources – to a more aesthetic interaction with the local environment, in which these same raw materials find their way into artistic expression. Some of Ransom's Fugitive/Agrarian colleagues took up the subject by hinting at how regionalism might mean more than just dressing up fiction with colourful local details. Robert

Penn Warren, for example, praised Southern writers who 'have not been content with the routine process of penetrating the surface of reported actuality,' but who instead strove to portray the South 'from the inside out' (*Southern Harvest* xvi); and Donald Davidson referred to the 'error' of 'assuming that the character of a regional art is determined principally by its subject matter, which must be local and special,' and suggested instead that critics might consider different modes of expression as evidence of distinct regional sensibilities (268).

Another persistent assumption stemming from regionalism's association with placid sketches of rural life is that it is not only aesthetically but also politically naive. Recent events in world politics belie this assumption, and a closer analysis of literary regionalism reveals that literature is not immune to regionalism's political tensions. Many of the authors examined in this study were active outside their literary careers in struggles against the hegemony of centralized political structures; if politics is considered in its broader sense, however, we can see that regionalism is politically active on multiple fronts. In examining borders that define difference, the regionalist author encounters confrontations not only along geographic borders that contain distinct local artefacts, but also along epistemological borders that define a particular sense of place, cultural borders that separate a distinct regional community from the larger society within which it exists, and aesthetic borders that define a distinct fictional world. On each of these levels, regional identity is constantly threatened by forces emanating from a larger world beyond its borders. The regionalist text is situated on these borders, and it is the regionalist's job to chronicle conflicts that shape a vital and evolving identity.

A comprehensive history of regionalist literature throughout the Americas from the early nineteenth century to the present day is beyond the scope of this study. Instead, my goal is a conceptual framework capable of accounting for a phenomenon that spans two continents and includes three linguistic and cultural heritages. In formulating a theory of New World regionalism, I have drawn on multiple sources, including literary theory, Hispanic studies, American studies, and various philosophical and theoretical approaches to textual analysis. I refer to examples of regionalist literature from Brazil, Mexico, the United States, and Canada. While each of these countries has a body of literature widely recognized as regionalist, the works I refer to are less commonly associated with the term 'regionalism.' Some are obscure works that have been neglected because of their regionalism; others are canonical texts that have been appreciated for reasons other than their regionalism.

CHAPTER ONE

A World Apart

SYMBOLIC REGIONS

The starting point in my study of New World regionalism is partly arbitrary: my attempts to trace the origins of regionalism in Brazil initiated a cycle of historical backtracking that I decided had gone far enough when it led me to a group of Brazilian poets writing in Paris in the early 1800s. But there are more cogent reasons for identifying the early nineteenth century as the beginning of New World regionalism, the first of which has to do with regionalism in general. Although literary accounts of local environments had existed for centuries in the form of travelogues and descriptive poetry, the fictional narrative set in a particular locality that we associate with regionalist literature began to develop only with the rising popularity of prose narrative fiction in the late eighteenth and early nineteenth centuries.

Another reason for starting my study at the beginning of the nineteenth century concerns New World regionalism in particular. Throughout the century, the fire of revolution that had begun in the previous century with the U.S. Declaration of Independence would spread sporadically through the countries of the Americas. The revolutionary atmosphere can be traced to multiple causes, including the spirit of freedom instilled by political philosophies of individual rights and the breakdown of feudal systems epitomized by the French Revolution. In the Americas, however, the spirit of rebellion had a distinct flavour stemming from a dawning recognition of isolation and difference.

Octavio Paz compares this recognition to the traumatic moment when as children we suddenly perceive our individuality, the moment at which 'between the world and ourselves a wall appears ... Something similar happens to countries in the process of growing up. Their being takes the form of a question: what are we and how do we realize that which we are?' (9). This moment of self-interrogation led many early nineteenth-century artists to turn their gaze away from Europe and towards their immediate environs. The transition was not an easy one: New World settings at first served mostly as ornamental trappings in which Old World stories were framed. Contradictory forces of assimilation and difference would render the use of indigenous New World material increasingly complex and problematic, but it was in this atmosphere of dawning self-awareness that New World regionalism was born.

New World authors struggling to express this new-found sense of selfhood were influenced by a romantic epistemology, the most commonly recognized characteristics of which include a break from the mechanistic world-view of the Enlightenment; an 'organic' view of nature as a living, dynamic web of 'correspondences,' or as an 'alphabet'; a reverence for nature, which was viewed as the conduit to humankind's divine origins; an 'aesthetics of genius' honouring the intuitive powers of the artist; and the perception of literary language and imagery as the symbolic representation of a transcendent harmony linking man and nature. Romantic poetics and epistemology would lead authors to neglect the tangible reality of New World environments and instead view New World regions symbolically as minor chapters in the greater history of human civilization.

The poetics of romanticism was influenced largely by German philosophy at the close of the eighteenth century, and in particular by the rising popularity of the human sciences.[1] In attempts to legitimate their own investigations, scholars in the late eighteenth and early nineteenth centuries adapted the methods and goals of the natural sciences to their investigations of human phenomena and substituted the social world of human interaction for the natural world of physical phenomena. This substitution is evident in early nineteenth-century New World regionalism, in which authors seemed more intent on assimilating descendants of the conquerors and settlers into a universal social world than on directly confronting the New World environment they inhabited. The social world that these regionalists emulated is best described by the German word *Bildung,* which, as Gadamer explains, had once been nearly synonymous with *Kultur,* or culture, but in early nineteenth-century usage came to emphasize *Bild,* or 'form,' and implied that culture meant 'cultivating' an ideal form (10–19). This romantic striving for an ideal human community is frequently cited by early New World regionalists as justification for conquest and settlement, and early regionalist texts portray regions as barren ground awaiting civilization's cultivating hand.

The rise of the human sciences in the early nineteenth century brought a new approach to the subject of enquiry. The phenomena observed by social scientists differ from those of the natural sciences in that examples must be taken from history, and history survives only insofar as meaning has already been imposed on events. Thus, as Gadamer concludes, in the social sciences, 'the primary data ... are not data of experiment and measurement, but units of meaning' (59). As a result, the humanist scholar's contact with the world of his or her investigation is not through sensory experience, but through intentional experience. Art came to be seen not as the representation of particulars of the contemporary reality, but as a symbolic representation of human experience in its entirety (Gadamer 63). This preference for human history over natural phenomena accounts for two persistent traits of early New World regionalism: a lack of descriptive detail, and a plethora of intertextual references to European culture.

The romantic epistemology that Gadamer describes strove for an assimilation of the individual to an ever greater unity: each experience contributed to an understanding of the whole of life, and each life strove towards integration with the human community to which it belonged. The effect on literature of this romantic yearning for transcendent unity is evident in a heightened regard for symbolism, often at the expense of allegory. Whereas the two had previously been more or less value-free, the symbol, because of its far-reaching referential capacity, was now considered better suited to the artistic pursuit of higher truths.[2] Despite some recent controversy over whether the symbol can be considered the defining trope of romanticism,[3] critics agree that romantics favoured figurative allusion over literal representation, and this preference for figurative language posed a considerable challenge for New World regionalists. Whether fiction strives for a transcendent unity or, as de Man argues, a deferral of presence, the linguistic and narrative strategies available to early nineteenth-century authors would seem to be antithetical to the portrayal of distinct geographic locales that is the basis of regionalism. The examples in the remainder of this chapter illustrate two responses to the challenge of romantic regionalism.

THE BRAZILIAN SERTÃO[4]

The conditions that led to the birth of New World regionalism were particularly pronounced in early nineteenth-century Brazil. António Cândido describes how in the early years of the century romanticism coincided with nationalism, and how both led Brazilian writers to an interest in local topics: 'In Brazil the romantic novel in its most typical examples ... portrayed reality through the point of view, the intellectual position, that affected all of our romanticism: that is to say, literary nationalism. Nationalism, in Brazilian literature, consisted basically of writing about local topics; in the novel, the immediate and fortunate consequence was the description of Brazilian places, scenes, facts, customs' ('Formação' 211). The convergence of romanticism, nationalism, and regionalism, Cândido concludes, gave rise to the origin of the Brazilian novel: 'The Brazilian novel was born with regionalism and the novel of customs' ('Formação' 113).

The origins of the regionalism that inspired Brazil's early novelists can be traced back to a group of Brazilian writers living in Paris in the 1830s. The combined influence of romanticism and nationalism is apparent in a letter that was published in the journal of the Historic Institute of Paris in 1834. The topic of the letter was the state of Brazilian culture in general, and one of the four contributors, Domingos José Gonçalves de Magalhães, dealt specifically with Brazilian literature. Magalhães expressed popular nationalist sentiment by suggesting that there might be found among Brazil's literature certain works that expressed a common spirit which distinguished Brazilian culture from that of Portugal. He went on to praise exemplary authors who had consistently treated local topics and who extolled patriotism and religion.[5]

In 1836, these expatriate Brazilian nationalists published a periodical entitled *Niterói, revista Brasiliense de ciências, letras, e artes,* and bearing the subtitle *Tudo pelo Brasil, e para o Brasil* (*Niterói, Brazilian Review of Sciences, Letters, and Arts; Everything for Brazil and by Brazil*). In the first of the review's two issues, Magalhães expanded on his theory of literary nationalism by linking national identity to literature: 'Can Brazil inspire the imagination of poets and have its own poetry? Its native inhabitants cultivate perchance poetry? The fact that the disposition and character of a country exercises a great influence on the physique and morale of its inhabitants is so well-known today that we take it as a principle, and deem it unnecessary to insist on demonstrating it with arguments and facts so naturally and philosophically exhibited' (Cited in Cândido, 'Formação' 13). Out of this short-lived association of expatriate Brazilian writers came a poem that would lead indirectly to the most significant body of romantic regionalist fiction to be produced in nineteenth-century

Brazil. In *A confederação dos Tamoios*, a poem commissioned by Emperor Dom Pedro II and published in 1856, Magalhães glorifies the indigenous peoples of Brazil. More significant than the poem itself is the response it elicited from a young author named José de Alencar, who attacked Magalhães's poem vehemently, criticizing various technical weaknesses, but above all decrying the ineffectiveness of Magalhães's meagre verses in the face of the epic subject the poem pretended to treat. Alencar's response would expand from a critique of other writers to his own indigenist fiction,[6] and finally to regionalist fiction and a theory of regionalism that would guide a century of Brazilian authors.

Not satisfied with criticizing Magalhães's poem through a series of published essays, Alencar decided to write his own epic poem, which he entitled *Os filhos de Tupã*. The title refers to the Tupi Indians, and in the poem's opening lines Alencar describes his goal as capturing the 'rough poem' or 'wild song' that would unite man and nature in a transcendent harmony. Alencar refers to the 'rough poem, the wild song, / of the sons of Tupã' (561), which he describes as Brazil's native song, emanating from the rough terrain of the country's natural landscape. *Os filhos de Tupã* was the beginning of his indigenist project and Alencar soon moved from writing poetry to prose fiction. In his first indigenist novel, *O guaraní*, Alencar expands on his theory of a national song emanating from the natural environment: a character in the novel contemplates the Indian language, wondering, 'Where did this uncivilized savage learn such a simple but graceful poetry?' (94–95). The character then realizes that this 'poetry' has its origins in nature: 'Brazilian nature, so rich and brilliant, was the image that this virgin spirit evoked, like the mirror of water reflects the blue of the sky' (95). Alencar initially saw indigenism as the answer to Brazil's need for an autonomous national literature: the country's pre-colonial indigenous culture would provide a uniquely Brazilian topic, and by portraying the Indian symbolically as the product of a land untainted by Western civilization Alencar would link contemporary Brazilian society to its origins in the natural environment of South America.

In response to criticism that the noble savage he portrayed in his indigenist novels had little to do with Brazilian reality, Alencar expanded on his nationalist theme by formulating a theory in the preface to his 1872 novel, *Sonhos d'ouro*, according to which indigenism would be just the first step in the development of a national literature. The preface begins with the author addressing his book in the second person, warning it of the prejudices it will encounter from Brazilian critics. Alencar then describes a more serious adversary that his book is bound to confront: European critics who, 'pitying our poverty, take it upon themselves to decide our fate and pronounce that we do not have, nor can we ever have, a Brazilian literature' (696). Of this class of critics, Alencar identifies two types: those who consider Brazil an 'empty nation' that 'does not have a native poetry, nor a flavour of its own' (696), and those who recognize a Brazilian literature, but want it to be exactly like the literature that existed in Portugal before the colonization of Brazil.

The seeds of Alencar's regionalism can be seen in his theory of the evolution of Brazilian literature. In his preface to *Sonhos d'ouro*, he asks rhetorically, 'What is the national literature but the soul of the native land, which populated this virgin ground with an illustrious race that infused itself with the American vitality of the land that served as a lap, and which each day is enriched through contact with other cultures and the influx of civilization?' (697). Here Alencar outlines three stages in the birth of a national literature: Brazil's national identity, as Alencar defines it, originates in the country's 'virgin ground'; the 'soul of the nation' was absorbed from the land by the country's indigenous inhabitants; and the literary expression of this national identity would finally be possible with the 'influx of civilization.'

Alencar elaborates on each of these three components, portraying them as steps in 'the organic period' of the development of a national literature (697). He calls the first step the 'aboriginal' phase, during which Brazil's early colonizers were subjected to the surviving traces of myths and legends of the conquered peoples, 'like the son whom the mother rocks in the cradle, singing songs of the lost country' (697). The second phase, which Alencar describes as 'historical,' encompasses the years between the arrival of European settlers and Brazil's declaration of political independence in 1822. This second stage is defined by 'the interaction between the invading people and the American land, which received from them culture, and in return offered the fruits of its virgin nature and the echoes of its splendid ground' (697). The third phase results from the interaction of 'the soul of the native land' and the 'influx of civilization' (697), and includes the time at which Alencar is writing: 'The third phase, the infancy of our literature, began with political independence and has not yet reached its conclusion; it awaits writers who will give it its final touches and will form the true national flavour' (697–98).

The single theme that dominates all these discussions of an indigenous national identity is the importance of land. From Magalhães's vague reference to 'the disposition and character of a country,' to the conflation of nature and indigenous culture in Alencar's indigenism, to the repeated emphasis on the influence of the 'wild land' in Alencar's theory of a three-phase cultural evolution, it was the New World environment that these writers believed would distinguish Brazilian society from that of its European founders.

Brazilian regionalism originated with Alencar's search for particular parcels of land that would be more conducive than others to the development of an indigenous culture; he alludes to these regions in his description of a 'native song' that embodies the soul of the society and that emerged during the second phase of his evolutionary scheme. This song is neither the myths and legends of conquered Indians, nor the polished music of advanced civilization, but the soul of the crude pioneer society, a song whose notes can be detected 'not only in the whispering breeze and the echoes of the forest, but also in the ballads of the people and the intimate hearths of the family' (698). Alencar maintained that this indigenous voice still survived in his time, but could be found only in isolated pockets protected from the rapid spread of civilization: 'Where the light of civilization, which suddenly alters the local colour, has not spread rapidly, there can still be found in its original purity, without adulteration, the simple life of our country – traditions, customs, languages – all with a totally Brazilian character. There are, not only in the country, but in the great cities and even the court, these hidden refuges that preserve the past almost intact' (698).

Specificity of place was an afterthought in Alencar's regionalism; in his first three regionalist novels these 'hidden refuges' where the 'simple life' of the country can still be found range from the southern plains to the interior of the state of São Paulo and to the northern state of Ceará. In response to continuing criticism of his lack of verisimilitude, however, with his fourth regionalist novel Alencar returned to the region he was most familiar with: the backlands of Ceará where he had grown up.[7] *O sertanejo* is the clearest expression of Alencar's desire to link cultural identity to specificity of place, and it also illustrates the problems posed by the contradictory requisites of romantic transcendentalism and regional specificity.

The opening sentence of *O sertanejo* introduces the regional subject of the novel: 'That immense plain, which extends toward unending horizons, is the *sertão* of my native land' (1019). Already, the novel illustrates at least two of regionalism's defining characteristics. First, the 'sertão' referred to is a well-defined geographic region. Second, because the

Ceará backland is in fact the 'native land' of the author himself, *O sertanejo* corroborates traditional definitions of regionalism as primarily autobiographical. Apart from its thematic content, the opening of *O sertanejo* also gives an indication of the romantic epistemology that informed Alencar's poetics: the description of the *sertão* is focalized through a position within the region, looking outward towards an infinite horizon. Although the three hundred or so pages that follow are dedicated to describing the region, the narrative perspective is always oriented towards that infinite horizon. Rather than investigate regional identity with the aim of enforcing regional autonomy, in *O sertanejo* Alencar strives to transcend borders, to assimilate the *sertão* with the rest of the country and ultimately with the European civilization of the country's founders. This outward-directed gaze reflects the romantic perception of the physical world as a mere vehicle towards a greater end: for Alencar, the physical region becomes merely a point of departure, not an end in itself. In Alencar's thematic references, language, and mode of narration, specificity of place constantly gives way to transcendent generalizations. The result is that the fictional world of Alencar's novel is a nebulous matrix that refuses to be contained within identifiable borders.

Alencar's nationalism consists mainly of attempting to prove not that Brazil is distinct from, but that it is *every bit as good as* the culture from which it was born. In *O sertanejo*, Alencar's method is to substitute the *sertanejo* for traditional heroes of European legend.[8] Arnaldo, the *sertanejo* of the novel's title, rescues Flora, the daughter of the plantation owner, for example, by leaping into a 'dragon of fire,' and, like the knight in shining armour of medieval legend, the leather-clad *sertanejo* fights 'hand to hand with the fire, giant against giant.' After his victory the *sertanejo* kneels and, taking a silver cross from around his neck, 'murmur[s] an Ave Maria, which he offered to the Holy Virgin in thanks for letting him arrive in time to save the damsel' (1028). In an overt reference to the Hercules legend, following another heroic rescue of Flora (this time from a rampaging bull), Arnaldo offers the damsel a bunch of coconuts 'as glorious as the golden fruits of the Hesperides' (1028).

The novel's narrated events are directed outward, not to an audience of *sertanejos* or even to a native Brazilian society, but to an audience conversant with European culture; a similar outward-directed gaze is reflected in the novel's language, which denies specificity of time and place. Events and objects that are nominally anchored in the northern *sertão* dissipate into a nebulous world that defies spatio-temporal specificity. After the novel's introductory passage, in which the first-person narrator reminisces about a childhood spent communing with nature, a specific temporal coordinate is given: lamenting the disappearance of the region's 'primitive roughness,' the narrator says, 'that is not how it was at the end of the last century,' and begins his narrative by describing 'the leader of the convoy who, on the tenth of December, 1764, followed the banks of the Sitía in search of the foothills of the Santa Maria Mountains, in the *sertão* of Quixeramobim' (1019). This spatio-temporal specificity quickly evaporates, however, when the narration shifts from 'esse momento' (the moment at which the travellers are traversing the plain) to a twelve-paragraph description of the landscape, a shift that is accompanied by a switch in verb tense, from the preterite tense of a specific historic moment to the present tense of a generalization lacking any temporal coordinates. Following the long present-tense description, the narration touches down briefly at that site along the riverbank once again, with a reference to 'the plain, which the travellers were traversing at that moment,' but then temporal specificity slips away as the sentence continues, 'had the desolate and profoundly sad aspect that these regions have in times of drought' (1021). Once again, after this brief reference to a particular region at a particular time, the narration digresses to generalizations about drought conditions, narrated in the present tense.

The transition from historic specificity to temporal generality is mirrored in a similar dissipation of specificity in character descriptions. In one passage, a group of characters at the head of the convoy is at first described through the focalization of someone within the convoy: 'Ahead of the convoy, and still very distant, was the cavalcade' (1020). The narrative focus then 'zooms in' to pick out particular individuals among this group: 'Among these, twenty belonged to a class that at the time had not yet become extinct: roughnecks that the landowners used as bodyguards and personal soldiers' (1020). With the introduction of these characters the narrative focus is already slipping towards generalization, away from specific ontological beings towards a general 'class.' In the next paragraph the pretext of a diegetic context is dropped altogether in favour of a generalized description: 'In general, these people wore suits in which the Portuguese style had been modified to adapt to the conditions of the *sertão*' (1020).

One of the main characters is introduced in the context of a specific time and place, but once again details give way to generalizations. The leader of the convoy is at first described in singular detail: a 'man of fifty, tall, robust complexion, demonstrating by the helmet and red scarf with gold that he was a captain of ordinance' (1020). But these specific traits recede into the background when the narrator intrudes with the observation that 'today we travel through the interior in riding clothes, but it wasn't the same in those days' (1021). With the transition from that day in December 1764 to 'those days,' the subject of the description shifts from *the* captain to *a* captain: 'a captain would consider it a disgrace if they were seen in the street, he and his wife, without the decorum his post required' (1021). Specific objects, characters, and events remain elusive throughout the novel, so that the fictional world of *O sertanejo* is only loosely tied to the physical world of northern Brazil. Although in his non-fiction Alencar introduced the notion crucial to New World regionalism that cultural identity could be derived from specificity of place, his fiction was not consistently regionalist. The *sertão* of Northern Brazil is only one of several regions he treated, and regionalism is only one among many of his literary projects. Alencar saw his role as similar to that of European romantic poets, but with a peculiar Brazilian adaptation: for the divine music of God's creation that the English romantics sought, Alencar substituted the native song of Brazilian national identity, a song symbolic not only of national unity, but of an even greater spiritual unity.

Alencar's preface to *Sonhos d'ouro* establishes the principles of early New World regionalism: its role in developing national identity, its ties to the natural environment, its source in isolated social communities, its role as an agent of historical conservation, and its predominantly rural character. The latter two principles account for much of the criticism to which regionalism would be subjected in years to come. Critics tend to congregate in urban centres and are often naturally indisposed to rural fiction, and regionalism's function as an agent of conservation, in addition to its autobiographic dimension, would mark regionalists as regressive and regionalist literature as more documentary than literary.

Alencar's most important contribution towards a definition of New World regionalist fiction is his emphasis on the intimate link between land and literature. Although Alencar's regionalism lacks the consistent specificity of place that would become crucial to later definitions, with his recognition of isolated 'refuges' he introduces the idea that certain areas are more conducive to the development of an autonomous cultural identity than others.

THE UNITED STATES PRAIRIE

Romanticism and nationalism were dominant forces in early nineteenth-century U.S. culture, but they did not produce the same widespread interest in regionalism that prevailed in Brazilian literature. In popular journals, essayists clamoured for an autonomous national identity, and, as in Brazil, the natural environment was seen as emblematic of the national spirit that authors strove to capture in literature. But whereas Cândido identifies attention to local detail in his description of the origins of the Brazilian novel, in romantic nationalist writing in the United States the one region that is most often singled out as emblematic of the American identity is praised not for its rich detail but for its emptiness. The open-ended opportunity sought by the American pioneers is frequently associated with the infinite horizons of the prairie.

Although Brazilians and Americans alike saw an intimate link between natural environment and national identity, Americans did not subscribe as enthusiastically to the primitivism that informed early Brazilian regionalism. In the United States, the natural landscape is typically described as barren, and its native inhabitants as similarly uncultivated, or barbarous. Thoreau typifies those who viewed the American landscape as a blank page awaiting the stamp of civilization when he describes the United States as a latter-day Eden, declaring that 'as a true patriot, I should be ashamed to think that Adam in paradise was more favorably situated on the whole than the backwoodsman in this country' (223). Thoreau links his optimistic projection for the founding of a new society to the grandeur of the American environment:

I believe that climate does thus react on man, – as there is something in the mountain air that feeds the spirit and inspires. Will not man grow to greater perfection intellectually as well as physically under these influences? ... I trust that we shall be more imaginative, that our thoughts will be clearer, fresher, and more ethereal, as our sky, – our understanding more comprehensive and broader, like our plains, – our intellect generally on a grander scale, like our thunder and lightning, our rivers and mountains and forests, – and our hearts shall even correspond in breadth and depth and grandeur to our inland sea. (222)

Thoreau's praise of the American terrain suggests that it is not any particular feature of their landscape that Americans saw as representative of their national identity, but rather the sheer immensity of it. Bernard Rosenthal describes Thoreau's description as typical, and in his survey of nineteenth-century travelogues, Rosenthal observes that despite their romantic adulation of nature, Americans were unusually inept at specifying the objects of their praise: 'That a litany of praise existed is certain, although to accept it at face value is to recover a nation that never quite existed. European travel writers visited a different nation, and, in their almost ritualistic comments on America's indifference to the beauties of nature, they fairly accurately portrayed America's aesthetics of nature' (46–47).

Nevertheless, early nineteenth-century American writers knew that a new and vital art could not come from inherited traditions; it could come only from direct contact with the New World that surrounded them. Emerson voiced the need to break away from tradition when he exhorted writers to seek 'an original relation to the universe': 'Our age is retrospective. It builds the sepulchres of the fathers. It writes biographies, histories, and criticism. The foregoing generation beheld God and Nature face to face; we through their eyes. Why should not we also enjoy an original relation to the universe? Why should not we have a poetry and philosophy of insight and not of tradition, and a religion by revelation to us, and not the history of theirs?' (7). Emerson's poetics, however, would inhibit the attention to local details and the recognition of difference that is essential to regionalism: although he encourages the writer to 'study with hope and love the precise thing to be done by him, considering the climate, the soil, the length of the day,' these specifics are merely a means to an end. Emerson's ultimate goal is not a distinct American reality, but a transcendent 'unconscious truth,' which is available only to one 'whose eye can integrate all the parts' (9). As with Alencar, Emerson's aesthetic and cultural goals do not focus on regional differences, but instead strive for a dissolution of the borders that define difference.

The American prairie suited the aims of both transcendent poetics and reverence for the country's natural grandeur. The view of the prairie as a landscape symbolic of American grandeur is expressed in Thoreau's association of the plains with a 'more comprehensive and broader' understanding, an association that would be echoed in the succeeding generation of poets by Whitman's reference to the prairies as the ideal source for 'a perfect poem, or other aesthetic work, entirely western, fresh and limitless' (863). Not only was the prairie typically American, but it was also suitably symbolic in the romantic sense of the term: only the 'limitless' prairie could encompass the 'integrity of impression' that Emerson sought. According to the prevailing view of humankind's place in the American landscape, the prairie would assimilate humankind and landscape by symbolically embodying the limitless aspirations of the American people.

Not only was the prairie seen as a symbol of America's infinite opportunity, but it also represented another kind of grandeur, one that can best be described as epic. The westward journey of the European settlers to the New World is often compared by nineteenth-century writers to the journeys of mythical heroes. Thoreau, for example, describes the sun as 'the Great Western Pioneer whom the nations follow,' and compares the United States to 'the island of Atlantis, and the islands and gardens of the Hesperides,' which he describes as 'the Great West of the ancients' (219). The pioneers' westward march across the prairies provides a narrative to accompany symbolic descriptions of the vast landscape, a narrative that is equally figurative in its allegorical associations.

Although most of the nineteenth-century American fiction that is preserved in today's popular culture is dominated by authors who lived in one particular place – the northeastern states – these authors showed little inclination to link identity to specificity of place. The titles of some of the best-known of these New England novels indicate an authorial gaze directed not to the immediate environs, but to the transcendent realm of symbolic correspondences: such titles as Hawthorne's *The Scarlet Letter*, or Melville's *Moby Dick*, for example, identify symbols as the works' central subjects. When James Fenimore Cooper came to write a novel entitled *The Prairie* he was not, despite the novel's title, concerned primarily with an investigation of particular details of regional identity. Instead, the prairie of the novel's title serves as a mythic realm in which a confrontation between the ideological forces of New World and Old is played out.

In *The Prairie*, Natty Bumppo, the American pioneer immortalized in Cooper's Leatherstocking tales, has fled the 'settlements' to live his final days on the 'borders,' or 'skirts,' of society. His tranquil domain is invaded by the family of Ishmael Bush, who, as his name suggests, is an outcast and wanderer. Plot is almost incidental in this novel: Bush's brother-in-law has kidnapped a Spanish heiress from a wealthy New Orleans family; the Bush clan push five hundred miles into the uncharted territory west of the Mississippi; then after several encounters with Indians, and a romantic subplot that unites two young couples, Bush condemns the kidnapper and turns the wagon train around, and the Bush clan rejoins society, leaving Natty to die in peace on the land that he knows and loves.

The terrain of Cooper's fictional world is not the United States we are familiar with: the centre, or 'bosom of the States' (68) lies on the eastern seaboard; the Mississippi is the western border, and beyond lies an uncharted tract referred to as 'the empty empire' (11). The literal referent is identified unambiguously through specific reference to the Louisiana Land Purchase of 1803, but in the world of Cooper's novel, the Mississippi River bisects a second, figurative landscape: to the east of the

Mississippi lies the familiar world of civilization, while to the west the rolling plains between the Mississippi and the Rocky Mountains represent an unnamed and unnameable void, described alternately as 'the bleak plain,' 'the seemingly interminable waste,' 'the endless wastes,' and 'the American deserts' (38, 77, 56, 40).

The narrator announces Cooper's unambiguous intention to cast Bush's trek through the empty prairie as a national epic depicting America's encounter with the New World: we are told that through the events narrated in this novel, we will be able to trace 'the march of civilization ... from the bosom of the States ... to those distant and ever-receding borders which mark the skirts and announce the approach of the nation as moving mists precede the signs of the day' (68). Whereas England is described as an empty hive, and the British as bees who 'flutter around the venerable straw,' claiming 'the empty distinction of antiquity,' the American pioneers are described as 'vigorous swarms that are culling the fresher sweets of a virgin world' (68).

Cooper's tale, however, is not the simple nationalist parable it first appears to be; underlying this straightforward march of progress is a profound sense of loss that contradicts the narrator's professed nationalist intentions. The events of the novel and the attitude of the narrator towards those events seem to condemn overwhelmingly the inexorable 'march of civilization' that is presaged by the Bush clan. The family's first encampment on the prairie hardly seems to champion any such notion of progress. The scene is narrated in starkly brutal terms: it begins when one of Ishmael's sons 'buried the ax to the eye in the soft body of the cottonwood tree'; the violence gains momentum as he 'quickly severed the trunk of the tree, bringing its tall top crashing to the earth in submission to his prowess,' and builds to a fury when, 'as if a signal for a general attack had been given,' his brothers 'stripped a small but suitable spot of its burden of forest as effectually and almost as promptly as if a whirlwind had passed along the place' (19).[9] The brutish pioneer justifies this rape of the land with his belief that 'the 'arth exists for our comfort' (23); Bush boasts that 'he had never dwelt where he might not safely fell every tree he could view from his own threshold' (69).

The novel's hero stands resolutely apart from this violent despoiling of the land. Natty witnesses the clearing of the campsite, and 'as tree after tree came whistling down, he cast his eyes upwards at the vacancies they left in the heavens, with a melancholy gaze, and finally turned away, muttering to himself with a bitter smile' (19). Later, Natty lashes out in anger: 'They scourge the very 'arth with their axes,' he exclaims, 'Such hills and hunting grounds as I have seen stripped of the gifts of the Lord, without remorse or shame!' (78). Natty has fled from civilization 'to escape the sound of the ax' (122), and is forever haunted by this sound: 'the wind seldom blows from the east,' he laments, 'but I conceit the sound of axes and the crash of falling trees are in my ears' (25).

The region's prior inhabitants seem to offer an agreeable alternative to the brutality of settlement. Despite the settlers' references throughout the novel to Indians as 'red devils,' 'barbarous and savage occupants of the country,' 'black-looking evil ones,' and so on (42, 14, 65), Natty clearly sides with the Indians, whom he describes as 'the rightful owners of the country' (28), and who live by 'the law of the prairie,' according to which 'the air, the water, and the ground are free gifts to man and no one has the right to portion them out in parcels' (82). The novel's closing chapter offers a dramatic contrast to the violence of the Bush encampment: as two settlers return to witness Natty's death in an Indian settlement, they are greeted by a pastoral scene: 'The sun was beginning to fall, and a sheet of golden light was spread over the placid plain ... Herds of horses and mules were grazing peacefully in the vast natural pasture under the keeping of vigilant Pawnee boys' (392). Here, where the region's 'rightful owners' live in harmony with the land, it seems that the venerable trapper has met his just reward; surrounded by a crowd of admirers gathered to pay homage to his years and his wisdom, Natty greets death with an equanimity suited to his peaceful surroundings.

At his death, Cooper's protagonist seems to be witness to a truly 'original relation to the universe' of the kind described by Emerson, born of the American prairie and lived by the region's 'rightful owners.' Yet despite all the evidence portraying whites as evil despoilers of the land, and Indians as the land's rightful owners, Cooper does not seem to consider adopting an indigenous 'prairie law' as a viable option. Natty turns a blind eye to the 'religion by revelation' (to use Emerson's phrase) evident in Cooper's description, and instead clings to tradition and history: 'You believe in the blessed prairies,' he tells his Indian friend, 'and I have faith in the sayings of my fathers' (399). At the climactic moment, Natty rejects a religion clearly in harmony with the land he loves so dearly, and chooses instead an imported set of beliefs clearly at odds with the New World environment.

Although Cooper's portrayal of characters and events seems to distance him from the settlers, his allegiance with the forces of civilization is evident in his use of language. Throughout the novel, names and naming

are portrayed as agents of colonization, no less alien to the region than
the sound of the axe. Yet even while ridiculing attempts to apply an alien
language to New World experience, Cooper himself becomes an unwitting accomplice to the linguistic colonization of the prairies.

Cooper ridicules attempts to affix Old World language to the New
World environment through the character of Dr Obed Bat, an itinerant
naturalist and physician who accompanies the Bush family. Armed with
magnifying glass and notebook, Bat is intent on classifying the contents
of the prairies, and his endeavours provide the novel's humorous
element. For example, when he stumbles across an animal in the night,
he rushes back to camp with the excited news that he has discovered a
new species, *Vespertilio horribilus americanus*. The animal wanders into the
camp, and Bat excitedly adds to his detailed observations, 'quadruped ...
ashy-plumbeous – no ears – horns, excessive,' but when the animal lets
out a familiar bray, Bat is crestfallen to discover that the beast is in fact
'*Asinus domesticus*,' or as Bush's daughter succinctly puts it, 'It is your own
ass' (75).

Similar incidents show how Bat's obsession with naming alienates him
from his New World surroundings. Bat has a running argument with
Natty concerning the difference between language and experience: in
one incident, Bat is reluctant to partake in a fireside feast while he
debates the name of the tasty morsel that Natty has offered him. He
insists that Natty must be wrong in identifying it as the hump of a buffalo
because the *Bos ferus* 'is not gifted with a hump at all' (104). As Bat
ponders Latin genera, Natty and his friend Paul Hover simply dig in to
a savoury meal that is described in sensuous detail.

In another scene, Natty derides the naturalist's practice of stuffing
animals, declaring that the 'worthless rags' have no relation to the living
prairie. The analogy between Bat's stuffed animals and his obsession with
words is clear: Bat's words – 'buffalo' or 'bison,' '*bos ferus*' or '*belluae*' –
are equally worthless representations of the prairie that surrounds them.
Natty makes the point clear when he tells Bat, 'Buffalo or bison, it makes
but little matter. The creatur' is the same' (80). Nevertheless, Cooper's
narrator contradicts Natty by siding with Dr Bat in authoritative footnotes
throughout the novel. For example, one note informs us that 'it is scarcely necessary to·tell the reader that the animal so often alluded to in this
book, and which is vulgarly called the buffalo, is in truth the bison'
(105).[10]

This authoritative stance is consistent throughout the novel; despite the
compelling contradictory argument offered by the novel's narrator and

its characters, Cooper himself consistently applies to his own rendering of the prairie the very practices that he ridicules in Bat. Cooper's use of footnotes mirrors Bat's practice by providing authoritative comments on American language and culture. In such explanations as 'The Americans call the autumn the "fall" from the falling of the leaf' (88), the narrator distances himself from 'Americans' by referring to them in the third person. Elsewhere, the narrator introduces American culture to a foreign readership with such explanations as 'The cant word for luggage in the Western states of America is "plunder"' (23), and 'Hominy is a dish composed chiefly of cracked corn, or maize' (21).

Not only does Cooper feel compelled to translate common American words and customs into formal English, but the entire novel is narrated in an inflated diction and convoluted syntax hardly less incongruous with the prairie environment than Bat's Latinate jargon. Although Natty, the region's resident naturalist, is confounded by the word 'incisors,' for example, later he has no trouble understanding Dr Bat's Latin. When Bat declares that 'the animals that are carnivorous are known by their incisors,' Natty responds dumbfoundedly, 'Their what?' (103); yet when, terrified by the darting eyes of a stampeding buffalo, Bat brands the beast '*Boves americani horridi!*' Natty replies, 'Aye horrid eyes enough' (211). When the narrator informs us that Bush speaks with his mouth full, we are told that 'the emigrant, who had, however, seen no apparent necessity to suspend the functions of his masticating powers, resumed the discourse' (23–24), and we see that the language of the novel's narration is no less inflated than the Old World diction that Cooper ridicules in Bat.

In addition to having incongruous language, the entire novel is framed in intertextual references to canonical British literature. Each chapter is prefaced with a quotation, usually from Shakespeare, but occasionally from other canonical authors. The epigraphs bear some nominal relation to narrated events: the second chapter, for example, in which Ishmael and his party break camp, finds its Shakespearean counterpart in a passage from *Richard the Third* that describes the pitching of a tent; and the cryptic 'Save you, sir' (attributed only to 'Shakespeare'; no work is cited) precedes a chapter describing Natty's escape from a hostile Indian band. More significant than their nominal relation to the narrated events, though, is the familiar frame these intertextual references provide for the unknown and unnamed prairie region in which the novel's events occur.

Unlike Alencar, Cooper did not simply transplant Old World stories to a New World setting. His descriptive details may be less than authentic,[11] but *The Prairie* attests to a real experience lived by Cooper and the preceding generation he describes. With the Old World behind him to the East and uncharted territory facing him to the West, Cooper seems to have recognized the same *mundo aparte* that Bolívar described in his 1815 'Carta de Jamaica.' This in-between state accounts for the almost spooky absence of presence in the narrated space of *The Prairie*. Characters occasionally wander out of the narrative spotlight to disappear 'in the fog of the prairies' (61), but apart from occasional references to a monotonous sea or a desert, descriptive details are limited almost exclusively to the characters themselves and whatever personal accoutrements lie within their reach.

Cooper's ambivalent portrayal of the American prairie – as both 'empty empire' and edenic garden – results from an inherent contradiction between his romantic and humanist ideals and the exigencies of regionalism. Despite his intuition that this region had a distinct culture defined by its relation to its natural surroundings, Cooper strove to define identity not as difference, but as similarity, and this longing for assimilation denied the possibility of portraying an autonomous regional identity. Despite his disdain for the British, Cooper ultimately frames the American prairie in a context more familiar to British readers than to American pioneers.

The contradictions between Cooper's thematic condemnation of settlement and his linguistic colonization of the prairie situate Cooper's text on an ambiguous ground. Cooper himself seems to have been unaware of the contradictions, but he unwittingly reveals an inherent characteristic of regionalism that later generations exploit more self-consciously. Some late twentieth-century regionalists have recognized that regional identity resides in borders that define difference, and have exploited postmodern techniques of deferring presence to portray a world defined by its borders. The generation immediately succeeding Cooper's reverses romanticism's outward gaze to focus more intently on the immediate details of Americans' contact with the New World environment, but the poetics of realism introduces some new challenges to authors investigating the effect of specificity of place on human identity.

CHAPTER TWO

Regions from Afar

HISTORICAL REALISM: FRANKLIN TÁVORA

In Brazil, as elsewhere in the New World, realism's demand for verisimilitude began to impose restrictions on the unfettered imagination of romantic novelists, and the primitivism of Alencar and others increasingly came under attack. In his article 'The Current State of Brazilian Literature: The Nationalist Instinct,' Machado de Assis recognizes the 'general desire to create a more independent literature' that had guided Brazilian authors throughout the nineteenth century, and summarizes Brazil's literature up to the three-quarter mark of the century as the attempt to express national identity through depictions of natural environment: 'Investigating Brazilian life and American nature, authors and poets find a fruitful source of inspiration and give the national thought its own physiognomy' (801–2). But Machado goes on to say that it is time for Brazilian authors to broaden their scope beyond local topics, and in particular to move beyond the primitivism that had become a national obsession. Machado does not advocate an outright abandonment of indigenous topics, but suggests that the glorification of Brazilian nature had outlived its usefulness as far as the development of a national literature was concerned.

Although Machado's cosmopolitanism was an exception among late nineteenth-century Brazilian literary critics, the feeling that such romantic regionalists as Magalhães and Alencar were outdated was widespread, and attacks on the previous generation's romantic idealism proliferated. In a series of letters appearing in a Rio de Janeiro journal in 1871, Franklin Távora vilified Alencar as an example of everything that was wrong with Brazilian literature.[1] He attacked Alencar's regionalism as 'mere fantasy,' and, in contrast to Alencar's 'closet literature' ('literatura do gabinete'), insisted that a true national literature can be derived only from direct observation of nature, not from imitation of inherited models: 'It is not isolated reading, even of the most carefully chosen models, that will give a faithful expression of nature. What is needed is to contemplate it, receive impressions face to face with the unknown; truly experience all the sensations of inspiration, not fictitious, but real' (Almeida 74). In seeking an alternative to Alencar's romantic abstraction, Távora cites James Fenimore Cooper as a model. Whereas Alencar writes *literatura do gabinete*, Távora says, Cooper 'sees first, observes, catches all the hues of nature, studies the sensations of the *I* and the *not I* ... and transmits it all with a photographic precision' (Almeida 73; Távora's emphasis). Távora's praise for Cooper's realism is somewhat ironic, since North American critics often fault Cooper for his questionable verisimilitude; nevertheless, Távora's comment alludes to a genuine difference between Alencar's regionalist writings and Cooper's Leatherstocking tales. Alencar drew his material almost entirely from European legend, whereas the contradictions underlying Cooper's depiction of the prairie attest to a more direct confrontation with the brutal reality of New World settlement.

An insistence on faithful observation of nature and verisimilitude in literature was of course not unique to Franklin Távora or to New World literature, but the poetics of realism would have specific implications for New World regionalism. Realism's separation of subject and object strove to transfer the locus of truth from the intentional world of human endeavour to the natural world. Realism's empirical approach tended to blur genre boundaries: taken to the extreme, it would result in regionalist novels that resembled catalogues of scientific data rather than narrative fiction. Towards the end of the nineteenth century, regionalism would display an affinity with naturalism, and adaptations of Zola's 'experimental method' would transform regions into laboratories in which the author would seek positivist explanations for regional identity.

Coinciding with the advent of realist aesthetics in the southern Americas was the shift in political self-awareness that António Cândido describes as a shift from 'consciousness of backwardness' to 'consciousness of underdevelopment' ('Backwardness and Underdevelopment' 263–5). What Cândido describes as the 'compensatory idealism' of early nineteenth-century regionalism resulted in picturesque literature that succeeded only in 'transforming the passion and suffering of rural people ... into an equivalent of pineapples and papayas' (278). Cândido observes that with the growing awareness of South America's political realities towards the end of the century, authors began to demonstrate 'a more realistic sense of the living conditions and the human problems of the forsaken groups' (280). Late nineteenth-century Latin American authors would use literature not only to depict the poverty in rural regions, but to justify it by portraying underdevelopment as the inevitable result of universal laws of social evolution.

Flora Süssekind elaborates on Cândido's examination of the role of realism by suggesting that in Brazil, realism and naturalism are inseparable. Obsessed by their need to find a unified national identity, Süssekind argues, Brazilian authors have always been attracted to naturalism because 'as an ideological discourse, naturalism is characterized by its covering up of division, of difference, and of contradiction' (39). Süssekind identifies three periods of crisis in Brazil's national identity from the late nineteenth century to the 1970s, and shows how in each case authors applied naturalist methods to indigenous topics in attempts to portray Brazil's shortcomings as regressive but necessary steps in an evolutionary dialectic.

The aesthetic and political consequences of the realism and naturalism that Cândido and Süssekind describe are illustrated in Távora's preface to his 1876 novel, *O cabeleira*. The preface begins by reiterating all the tenets of romantic regionalism outlined by Alencar, but then shifts suddenly to describe a new regionalism, one shaped by the combined effects of realist aesthetics, political self-consciousness, and naturalist determinism. Like Alencar, Távora describes his objective as a truly Brazilian literature; he stresses the importance of land, and suggests that certain regions – the North of Brazil in particular – retain significant traces of an indigenous culture: 'Literature, like politics, has a certain geographic character; but in the North, more than in the South, can be found the elements for the formation of a distinctly Brazilian literature, born of the earth. The reason is obvious: the North, unlike the South, is not being subjected to the daily invasion of foreign influences' (15). The personal attachment to a particular region that underlies all regionalism is even more explicit in Távora than in Alencar. Just as an affinity for his 'native land' had led Alencar back to Ceará in *O sertanejo*, so his regional loyalty leads Távora to refer to Pernambuco, the province he was raised in, as 'that shining star of the Brazilian constellation' (12) and to describe the region in hyperbolic terms:

Entering there I seem to be entering a fantastic temple of infinite proportions. It is only natural: whenever we find ourselves before the masterpieces of creation, a secret instinct warns us that we are in the presence of God. Admiration then takes on the solemnity of a meditation and an homage. Impressions pass from the senses to the depth of the soul where they are repeated with greater intensity. All our faculties – intelligence, imagination, even our will – are dominated by something like a voluptuousness that is not sensual, but delightful, an overwhelming ecstasy. Even when our spirit is tired of the faults and injustices of man, it is immediately lifted, full of life before the enormous representation, as if it encounters itself in its virginal integrity. (13)

Távora's reverence for his native region reflects what seems to be a typically romantic approach to regionalism: that contemplation of the region's limitless natural beauty will enable one to transcend the 'faults and injustices of man' and find the 'virginal integrity' of the soul mirrored in God's creation. The tone of Távora's preface changes suddenly, however, when the author considers what effect industrialization might have on the region: 'It would not be the same world – I thought, descending from the heights of contemplation to the plains of positivism, if cities rose up along these banks' (15). Távora then describes a utopian vision of a future in which the 'dark forest' and 'black, barren fields of hunger' would be replaced by 'magnificent emporiums' of commerce and industry, and he jubilantly declares that 'at each turn would be a Manchester or a New York' (15).

Such an enthusiastic endorsement of urbanization contradicts traditional definitions of regionalism, but it is typical of late nineteenth-century New World regionalism. Confronting the political reality of their surroundings, authors saw that the pastoral paradise envisioned by romantics had not materialized. Távora's strategy is to portray the region as a repository of natural resources awaiting what he refers to as the 'next phase,' in which the 'brilliant landscape of virgin nature' would be replaced by 'magnificent emporiums' of commerce. Unlike the narrator of Alencar's *O sertanejo*, who from his internal perspective sought to dissolve the borders separating region from world, Távora views the region from afar and envisions not a dissolution of the centre/margin dichotomy, but a displacement of the centre, a shift of political and economic power from São Paulo and Rio de Janeiro in the South to new centres in the North.

In *O cabeleira*, Távora chooses for his subject a theme that is popular in northeast Brazil's folk tradition: the roving bandits (or *cangaceiros*) who often took refuge in the backlands of the Northeast, and would be immortalized in folk legend as outlaw heroes for their defiance of political authority housed in urban centres to the south. Távora describes the adventures of one such outlaw, known popularly as Cabeleira (roughly translated, Cowboy), who is purported to have roamed those backwoods in the late eighteenth century.

Távora adopts the conventions of the historical novel in an attempt to establish securely this hero's place in Brazilian history. Távora's choice of genre would seem to contradict his edict that fiction must proceed from direct observation of the natural world, but he identifies his sources as popular ballads and 'a few lines of history' (19) and accords them the same unimpeachable veracity as natural objects. By limiting the world of his novel strictly to material drawn from these sources, Távora distances himself from the novel's subject and lays claim to mastery over a complete and knowable world. The author's privileged perspective is reflected in the narrator's introduction of the protagonists in the novel's opening pages: 'God alone knew the three adventurers ... the past that condemned them, the future that awaited them' (30). Távora lays claim to a similar God-like omniscience when he declares in a concluding postscript that 'Cabeleira is not a fiction, is not a dream, he existed, and he ended up just as I have described' (193).

Any historical novel is constrained by what Brian McHale describes as 'historical realemes,' a term he uses to designate 'persons, events, specific objects, and so on [that] can only be introduced on condition that the properties and actions attributed to them in the text do not actually contradict the "official" historical record' (97). Ordinarily, McHale explains, the author of historical fiction is offered a certain leeway for invention by ' "dark areas" of history, that is ... those aspects about which the "official" record has nothing to report' (87). Távora, however, attempts to deny the existence of any such 'dark areas,' and treats historical record as a natural object, complete in and of itself and knowable in its entirety. The result is a fictional world that is highly detailed in its exaggerated temporal and spatial specificity, but at the same time severely limited by its strict adherence to historical record. For example, by using only available historical 'facts,' the physical setting of a scene in which Cabeleira and his two companions arrive in Recife is limited to a single verifiable historical object – a bridge – which is presented in excruciating detail, from the date of its construction and the names of its architect and of the governor who commissioned it, to the materials of its construction. We are told that stores lining the bridge's sides were commissioned by Governor Henrique Luís Vieira Freire de Andrade so that he could collect a rent of eight hundred *mil reis*, which would finance the restoration project of bridges throughout the province; that the bridge's wooden archways dated back to the Dutch influence that dominated such architecture in the late eighteenth century; and that the bridge's stone foundations survived from a previous bridge, the architect and commissioning governor of which are also identified by proper name (*O cabeleira* 20–9).

While the avowed separation of the author from his subject leaves Távora little leeway in the construction of the novel's fictional world, it permits the inclusion of a commentary emanating from the perspective of a detached authority, and Távora uses this perspective to support his regionalist argument. Readers are advised at the novel's outset that the life of Cabeleira contains 'a big lesson' (19), and throughout the novel the narrator interprets the significance of the narrated events. As the novel progresses, the author's didactic intention becomes clear: Cabeleira's life of crime is attributed to conditions that parallel the backwardness of the North in Távora's time, and his execution is equated with injustices emanating from the country's centralized power structure.

The narrator presents Cabeleira as the victim of forces beyond his control and goes on to blame injustices perpetrated by the South against the Northeast for these forces. He explains that among the neglected heroes of the country are 'unfortunate figures who would today be venerated as models of virtue, if certain circumstances of time and place ... had not succeeded in disfiguring men, making them tormentors of their own generation and even turning them into their own executioners. Among these is the protagonist of the present narrative, who led a celebrated career of crime, less by natural evil than by the crass ignorance that in his time enslaved good instincts and freed the cannibal passion' (19). These 'cannibal passions' are repeatedly cited as the source of violent or cruel actions committed by the novel's characters, and the 'lesson' Távora draws is that this ignorance is due to the region's neglect at the hands of a distant political capital. For example, when Cabeleira's father kills one of the fleeing villagers, readers are told that the character's violence is due to the 'shadow of ignorance' the backwoodsman lived in, which had 'extinguished in him the light of rational conscience that all men carry with them from birth' (27). And when a soldier dies in pursuit of Cabeleira, we are told that the reckless pursuit that resulted in his death is 'motivated more by a surge of passion than by a conscious devotion to duty' (28). Implicit in all these references to backwoods ignorance is the condemnation of a centralized system that has failed to 'civilize' these marginal communities.

Távora's political motives become explicit when the novel's 'lesson' is finally spelled out at the end, with the explanation that not only was Cabeleira's life of crime the result of ignorance rather than conscious intent, but Brazil's centralized society was to blame for his ignorance: 'Justice executed Cabeleira for crimes that had their principal origin in ignorance and poverty. But isn't the cause of similar injustices above all a society that does not fulfil its obligation to spread instruction, the source of morality, and to organize work, the source of wealth?' (191). Cabeleira's ignorance is blamed on the marginal status conferred on him by a centralized society, and this marginalization mirrors the backwardness of the North Távora describes in his preface: 'If capital and credit were mobilized, if agricultural, industrial and artistic markets were put in place, we would see at every turn a Manchester or a New York ... Work, capital, economy, abundance, wealth, indispensable agents of civilization and greatness would take a prominent place in the immense expanse' (15).

O cabeleira demonstrates the interdependence of politics and aesthetics that Cândido and Süssekind describe. The region is seen from afar as an autonomous object; the narrator's distant perspective and strict adherence to historical record result in a clearly circumscribed fictional world. Unlike Alencar's romanticism, which strove for the dissolution of the borders separating region from world, Távora's realism is intent on erecting rigid borders defined from the external perspective of empirical observation.

It is clear from Távora's preface and from the didactic 'lesson' of his novel that he strove not to assimilate the margin to the centre as Alencar did, but to displace the centre and make the Northeast a new 'emporium of commerce.' Távora believed not only that his novel's 'lesson' would contribute to a realignment of political power, but that his regionalism would contribute to a corresponding realignment of cultural authority. Távora devoted his entire literary career to a regionalist project he called 'a literatura do Norte,' and he said that his aim was 'to construct a literary edifice' (16). The 'edifice' Távora envisions is an aesthetic monument capable of displacing the cultural authority of the South that was enshrined in literary anthologies, intellectual journals, and national museums.

Távora was a transitional figure in the development of Brazilian regionalism. While his attack on romanticism and his regionalist politics constitute an important contribution to the development of literary regionalism, his fiction itself is a rather clumsy attempt at integrating regionalist politics with realist and naturalist aesthetics. Realist regionalism would be refined in more artful infusions of politics and aesthetics by such late nineteenth-century Brazilian authors as Domingos Olympio, Manoel de Oliveira Paiva, Inglez de Sousa, and Rodolfo Teófilo. Brazilian naturalism would reach its culmination in Euclides da Cunha's *Os sertões,* a book that defies genre classification, but represents a climactic amalgamation of all the principles of New World regionalism developed gradually over the course of the century: from Magalhães's suggestion that a unique New World environment might influence the character of its inhabitants, to Alencar's three-part theory involving an integration of land, indigenous peoples, and civilization, to Távora's insistence on historical verisimilitude.

NATURALISM AND REGIONALISM: EUCLIDES DA CUNHA

After a long career as a military engineer and occasional journalist, Euclides da Cunha was working as a civil engineer in São Paulo when, in 1896, reports of a rebellious uprising in the backlands of northern Brazil reached the country's capital. When a military expedition was sent to disperse the group of religious fanatics who, following the counsel of backwoods messiah António Conselheiro, had erected a fortified stronghold in Canudos, Cunha was commissioned by a São Paulo newspaper to accompany the expedition. Cunha explains in the preface to *Os sertões* that in the five years that lapsed between the defeat of Conselheiro's followers and the publication of his book, he revised his manuscript, 'giving it a new form,' so that what had begun as a journalistic record of the military campaign became a sociological treatise, aimed at analysing the 'significant present-day characteristics of the subraces to be found in the backlands of Brazil' (xxxi). Cunha's expansive examination of the northeastern *sertão* and the region's influence on its resident *sertanejos* was in fact the crowning achievement in a century of regionalist literature that had begun with Magalhães's vague intuition that the New World environment might influence 'the physique and morale' of its inhabitants.[2]

It is easy to understand why, nearly a century after its publication, *Os sertões* is still the subject of a heated literary debate. Written by a mechanical engineer moonlighting as a journalist, and described by its author as a sociological study, *Os sertões* is of considerable interest to sociologists, historians, and geographers, as well as to literary critics. The result of Cunha's diligent research and meticulous observation is treated for the most part as an oddity by members of the literary community. The most obvious reason for its ambivalent reception is the author's own insistence that *Os sertões* is not a literary work of art, but a scientific treatise, the write-up of an experiment in which the Northeast served as an extended laboratory. Another compelling, though often unstated, reason for critics' uneasiness with Cunha's work is the unfortunate racism inherent in the Darwinist approach that informs his methodology.

Perhaps the most compelling argument against the inclusion of *Os sertões* in a literary canon is formulated by Luis Costa Lima, who calls on an impressive repertoire of philosophical sources, from classical theories of mimesis to Freud's theory of identity, in support of his exclusion of *Os sertões* from the realm of literary art. Intentionality lies at the centre of Costa Lima's argument: he declares that a discourse can be considered literary fiction only when it displays an array of images that are 'thematized by the imagination' (47). It is an inconsistency of thematization in one of *Os sertões*'s sections, Costa Lima argues, that disqualifies Cunha's work as literary art. Costa Lima argues that a 'tragic, agonistic sense of the land ... functions as the principle of selection for Cunha's mimesis' (185), but only in two of the book's three divisions. Therefore, Costa Lima concludes, the thematic unity in *Os sertões* 'is a subordinate presence, for another form of tragedy, one having nothing to do with mimesis outweighs it' (185). Costa Lima calls this other form of tragedy 'the tragedy of impasse' (185), and attributes it to the author's inability to impose closure of meaning on the material he selected for the book's second section. Defining the role of the author by his or her function of 'mimetizing' observed phenomena, Costa Lima describes the middle section of *Os sertões* as the result of a 'confrontation with an other so different that the mimetizable agent – the author – rejects it and takes it as unorganized, unbalanced, and retrograde' (185).[3] His conclusion is that although two of *Os sertões*'s three divisions can be considered literary, the work as a whole cannot: 'Since the tragic-agonistic shares power with the tragic-of-impasse, or, better, since the former results from the organizing principle of the work whereas the latter derives from the fact that a given theoretical schema cannot adequately account for its object without in the process leading to another schema, it becomes improper to speak of *Os sertões* as a work of fiction' (185).

Os sertões may not be a literary work of art according to classical definitions of tragedy or mimesis, but considered in light of the sense of place that informs a regionalist aesthetic, it is a literary masterpiece. Cunha's work is certainly not fictional in the way that, for instance, Alencar's *O sertanejo* is, and Costa Lima's analysis provides sound theoretical justification for the uneasiness that a lot of critics might feel when the work is placed alongside the more clearly novelistic works of Alencar or Távora. *Os sertões* does, however, exhibit undeniable evidence of novelistic fictionalization and dramatization of observed phenomena, and furthermore, when the book is considered as a work of regionalist literature, the middle section can be seen not as evidence of inconsistent fictionalization, but as a crucial part of a unified narrative depicting the effect of specificity of place on human identity.

The organization of *Os sertões* reflects the premises that had shaped a century of Brazilian regionalism: that the natural environment of the New World is the source of an autonomous cultural identity; that the primitive inhabitants of remote regions embody the characteristics of the New World environment; and that the confrontation between these primitive people and urban society would result in the integration of Brazilian nature with Western civilization. The three sections that Costa Lima describes as disjunctive in fact represent a dramatization of Alencar's three-part theory of regionalist evolution: part one, 'The Land,' portrays the region's geological formation as the source of a distinctive regional identity; part two, 'The Man,' describes the *sertanejo* as a primitive race susceptible to environmental influences; and part three, 'The Rebellion,' portrays the military suppression of the Canudos uprising as the forced integration of primitive man with advanced civilization.

Whereas realist epistemology had been implicit in Távora's regionalist aesthetics, Cunha consciously applies to regionalism not only the realist reliance on objective observation, but also naturalism's goal of deriving incontrovertible conclusions through deductive reasoning. Whereas Zola had lamented in 'The Experimental Novel' that 'we have not yet reached the point of being able to prove that the social milieu also is nothing but chemical and physical' (174), Cunha aims for precisely such a reduction. In his attempt to reduce the Canudos campaign to a controlled sociological experiment aimed at tracing regional identity to its organic sources, Cunha admits that the 'complex biological reactions' between humankind and environment involve 'more energetic agents than for the chemical reactions of matter' (67), but he believes that these 'agents' can be identified and subjected to empirical analysis just as the components of simple chemical reactions can be isolated: 'To heat and light, which exert their influence in both cases, there is added the lay of the land, the climatic manifestations, and that undeniable presence, that species of mysterious catalytic force, which is immanent in the various aspects of nature' (67). The last of these 'agents,' the 'mysterious catalytic force' exerted by a specific place on its inhabitants, is the source of regional identity, the nebulous 'substance' that traditional definitions of regionalism refer to.[4] This mysterious ingredient poses a problem for Cunha's empirical method, for it is not immediately accessible to the author's analytic gaze. Cunha is confident, however, that deductive reasoning will finally reveal this essential substance of regional identity; his reference to its 'immanence' in such quantifiable phenomena as heat, light, topography, and climate implies that once all of these are measured and recorded, the 'mysterious force' will be unveiled.

Cunha reiterates the importance of place by adopting naturalism's emphasis on environment's effect on humanity, and his Darwinist theory of social evolution aims to justify the theory voiced by both Alencar and Távora that the North in particular is the true birthplace of an authentic Brazilian culture. According to Cunha's theory, while European settlers prospered in the 'luxuriant and easily accessible regions' of the South, 'the northerner did not possess a physical environment which endowed him with an equal amount of energy' (66). Cunha concludes that the harsh climate weakened the racial stock of settlers in the North, and that this weakened race then absorbed characteristics of the three dominant races (European, African, and indigenous peoples). The result was what Cunha describes as a new 'subrace,' which, although weakened, would bear the stamp of its natural environment:

The juxtaposition of characteristics means an intimate transfusion of tendencies; and the corresponding long period of transformation is by way of being a period of debilitation so far as the capacities of the crossed races are concerned; all of which increases the relative importance of the influence of environment. Environment is then, as it were, better able to stamp its own characteristic features upon the human organism in process of fusion. (67)

This Darwinist explanation provides an explicit illustration of Süssekind's theory concerning the Brazilian application of naturalism. Cunha describes the 'period of debilitation' resulting from miscegenation as only a temporary setback; he is confident that the resulting race will eventually be reintroduced to civilized society, bringing with it the 'stamp' of the regional environment.

Cunha's own approach to the region is reflected in his depiction of a character who views the *sertão* with detached curiosity: 'This highly original landscape held an attraction for him. Its strange flora, its extremely rugged topographical outlines, its geognostic structure – which has not yet been studied – all this lay before him, all around him, a turbulent chapter in the history of Earth which no one as yet had read' (295). Like Távora, Cunha relies on objective observation, but Cunha substitutes the natural world for the historical record that Távora had relied on; just as history books had provided Távora with a complete and knowable reality, objective firsthand observation would render the *sertão* an open book to Cunha's analytic gaze. By denying intentionality, Cunha attempted to close the ontological gap between book and world; for him the author's role was that of a knowledgeable reader who could transcribe the 'book' that lay before him directly into the pages of the book that he was now presenting to his readers.

This denial of intentionality is accepted at face value by critics arguing against the literary artistry of *Os sertões*. The author's claim to objective observation, however, is contradicted by his obvious fictionalization and dramatization of observed data. Cunha exhibits a distinctly novelistic trait in his transformation of generic descriptions into singular fictional characters. His description of a typical *sertanejo*, for example, might be constructed from a composite of actual, observed traits, but has no single, identifiable referent in the world of the author and reader:

He is ugly, awkward, stooped. Hercules-Quasimodo reflects in his bearing the typical unprepossessing attributes of the weak. His unsteady, slightly swaying, sinuous gait conveys the impression of loose-jointedness. His normally downtrodden mien is aggravated by a dour look which gives him an air of depressing humility. On foot, when not walking, he is invariably to be found leaning against the first doorpost or wall that he encounters; while on horseback, if he reins in his mount to exchange a couple of words with an acquaintance, he braces himself on one stirrup and rests his weight against the saddle. (89)

The 'Hercules-Quasimodo' described by Cunha is no less fictional than the protagonists of any of Alencar's novels.

Cunha exhibits a similar tendency to fictionalize in his narrative passages by drawing on a number of observed historical events in order to invent a single fictional event. His description of the region's annual cattle stampede, for example, begins with what is presumably a statement of fact drawn from personal observation: 'the cow-hunt ... consists essentially in first rounding up and then separating the cattle of the various neighbouring ranches' (98). This general observation then gives way to a single narrated event: 'Of a sudden, however, a concerted shudder runs through the herd, over those hundreds of glossy backs. There is an instantaneous halt. Hundreds of pairs of horns then clash and lock, are tossed in the air writhing and twisting' (100). The details of this narrated event may in fact be taken from a single observed event, a technique reflecting the author's intentionality only through its use as a representation of multiple similar events. Cunha's intentionality is more evident in other narrative passages that are more clearly fictionalized. In one such example, what begins as a general description of the *caatinga*, or backlands scrub-brush, and its importance in the military tactics of the *sertanejo* soon becomes dramatized in a purely invented battle:

With all this, the caatingas are an incorruptible ally of the sertanejo in revolt, and they do in a certain way enter into the conflict ...

Suddenly, from the side, close at hand, a shot rings out. The bullet whizzes past them, or perhaps one of their number lies stretched on the ground, dead. This is followed, after a while, by another, and another, whining over the heads of the troop ... It is then that a strange anxiety lays hold of even the bravest ones whose courage has many times been put to the test. (190–91)

The author's use of 'perhaps' attests to the passage's fictionality; his reference to the soldiers' 'strange anxiety' indicates the inclusion of subjective interpretation. As in Alencar's fiction, such present-tense narratives bring to the surface the ontological boundary separating real-world events from those of the work's fictional world. Cunha's use of iterative narrative denies the possibility of a direct one-to-one correspondence between the narrated events of *Os sertões* and the actual historical events he had originally set out to chronicle. Like his fictional characterization of the *sertanejo*, these narrated events have no real referent in the *sertão* of northern Brazil.

In addition to fictionalizing and dramatizing his observations, Cunha exhibits a novelistic penchant for narrative. In places, *Os sertões* reads like the scientific record of empirical fact that it purports to be – as in the reference to the *sertão* as 'a region in which the thermometric and hygrometric readings, marked by exaggerated extremes vary in inverse ratio' (55) – but at other times, even descriptions of inanimate objects are woven into a narrative that testifies to an imagination no less fecund than that of Alencar. A description of the sparse vegetation, for example, becomes a dramatization of 'the agonized struggles of a tortured, writhing flora' engaged in a 'silent battle' with the harsh environment (30, 31). And even geological formations become animated in a historical drama:

Then the lands of the far north of Baía, represented by the quartzite rocks of

Monte Santo and the summits of Itiuba ... began a continuous ascent, with an increase of visible bulk. But in the course of this slow rise, while the highest regions, only recently raised above sea-level, were sprinkled with lakes, the entire middle portion of this promontory remained immersed. An impetuous current ... held it in its grip. Beating against it for a long time ... the mighty current continued working on this corner of Baía, until, in accordance with the general movement of the lands, the region had wholly emerged and had become the shapeless heap of mountainous ruins that it is today. (16–17)

Although Cunha's fictionalized and dramatized descriptions and narratives may add up to a convincing account of conditions in the northern *sertão*, they contradict the author's claim that regional identity can be captured in purely empirical observation of natural phenomena.

Each of the nineteenth-century Brazilian authors we have looked at so far thought he knew where he could find the 'substance' of regional identity: Alencar thought it resided in a song that could be heard only by poets; Távora sought it in the pages of history; and Cunha thought it lay hidden in the topography and climate of the *sertão*. From Magalhães to Cunha, authors called for increasing reliance on empirical detail in attempts to reduce or abolish the 'dark areas' in their fictional worlds. The attempt was taken to its extreme by Távora, who attempts to reduce regional identity to a detailed catalogue of names, dates, and economic data. The shortcomings of such an empirical approach to the investigation of regional identity are illustrated by Cunha, who, despite his professed reverence for objective disinterest, seems impelled to resort to fictionalization and dramatization in his attempt to catalogue the sources of regional identity. Cunha's recourse to imagination and invention suggests that the 'mysterious catalytic force' he sought may not reside entirely in the empirical objects that realist authors sought to classify and enumerate. Meanwhile, regionalist authors in the United States had confronted the same inherent contradiction between regionalism's 'mysterious force' and realism's pragmatic observation and deduction.

LOCAL COLOUR: WILLIAM DEAN HOWELLS AND HAMLIN GARLAND

In the latter decades of the nineteenth century the westward trek of civilization across the United States that Cooper described in *The Prairie* had reached its terminus at the Pacific Ocean. The prairie was being tilled and cities were rising on the Pacific coast. The vast terrain of the continent, which had once inspired visions of symbolic unity, was now seen more as a conglomerate of isolated local realities. Regionalist fiction proliferated in the latter decades of the nineteenth century, and its popularity was largely due to William Dean Howells; perhaps the single most influential author, critic, and editor in American literature at the time, Howells exhorted authors to turn to their immediate environments for material for their fiction. Howells believed that the detailed examination of local settings would produce a distinctive American style, and that together these regionalist works would gradually fill in a unified portrait of a distinct American culture.

To Howells, realism, regionalism, and nationalism were inseparable. Declaring that in order for American culture to break free from its British ancestry 'the arts must become democratic,' he praised authors who chronicled the daily lives of the common citizen (66). He described the careful observation of local details as a 'vertical' examination of national character, which he opposed to the 'horizontal' sweep of heroic fiction typical of such British writers as Sir Walter Scott (67). Howells had a particular vision of the national character that would emerge from such a 'vertical' examination of the American environment: comparing America's 'rarefied and nimble air full of shining possibilities and radiant promises' to 'the fog-and-soot-clogged lungs of those less-favored islanders,' he was certain that verisimilar depictions of local environs would produce a cheerful image of the national character (61, 62). In the late 1880s, an economic depression and violent labour conflicts would cause Howells to re-examine this cheerful image of American democracy, but this re-examination would not alter his belief that accurate descriptions of isolated regions would gradually fill in a unified portrait of American identity.

According to Howells's realist poetics, regionalism, and even the nationalism he so ardently championed, was the means to a greater end. The local details that he exhorted authors to capture would lead to a distinctive American literature, and this literature in turn would contribute to the ultimate goal of all art: the discovery of a universal truth that transcends differences between individuals. Howells's nationalism grew from his conviction that the American environment was uniquely suited to the accomplishment of this goal: 'Men are more like than unlike one another,' he declared, and the aim of all fiction is to 'make them know one another better, that they may all be humbled and strengthened with a sense of their fraternity' (87). Thus, although he believed that the

American environment provided a unique subject for authors, to Howells, 'the truth is deeper and finer than aspects,' and details of local colour are therefore merely coincidental.

Hamlin Garland was a devoted protegé of Howells, and an enthusiastic champion of his call for realism and regionalism in literature. In his 1892 collection of essays, entitled *Crumbling Idols*, Garland echoed Howells's demand for a new literature that would not only break away from romantic idealism, but challenge outdated notions of cultural homogeneity. The 'idols' referred to in the title of his collection are such monuments of Western culture as the works of Homer and Shakespeare, which Garland describes as landmarks littering 'a highway of dust.' As Garland sees it, American authors had been following this 'highway' blindly, spurred on by aged critics who found comfort in the past: 'Old men naturally love the past; the books they read are the master-pieces; the great men are all dying off, they say; the young man should treat lofty and universal themes, as they used to do' (63). It is by clinging to this outdated notion of universality, Garland claims, that American writers perpetuate literary colonialism. While such themes may provide comfort to aged critics, he argues, they are irrelevant to American literature: 'It has taken the United States longer to achieve independence of English critics than it took to free itself from old-world political and economic rule ... Our writers ... rested their immortality upon the 'universal theme,' which was a theme of no interest to the public and of small interest to themselves' (60). As long as American authors attempt to perpetuate ideals that originate in a past that is not their own, American literature will stagnate. 'Life means change,' Garland insists, and he argues that a vibrant literature must derive its force not from similarity and assimilation, but from change. A healthy literature must therefore strive not for universality, but for difference, and difference can be found only in material close at hand: 'Local color ... is demonstrably the life of fiction. It is the native element, the differentiating element ... It is the differences which interest us; the similarities do not please, do not forever stimulate and feed as do the differences. Literature would die of dry rot if it chronicled the similarities only' (57).

Garland's emphasis on difference may have a familiar sound to today's readers of Foucault or Derrida, but the 'difference' he refers to is quite distinct from our postmodern understanding of difference. It is not change itself that interests Garland, but its effects: difference for Garland does not mean a deferral of presence, or the perpetuation of indeterminacy, but rather a succession of frozen images. History, for the realist author, was a progression of discrete moments, each of which could be frozen in the pages of narrative fiction, and difference meant the comparison of one static portrait to another. The novelist's task, as Garland describes it, is to study phenomena that are unified by their inclusion in a temporal frame distinguishing the present from other discrete time segments: 'The past is dead,' Garland asserts, 'and the future can be trusted to look after itself' (79). What is left is the present, and for Garland the present is accessible to the author in all the local details that surround him.

Garland differed from Howells in one key respect: unlike his literary mentor, he maintained a personal attachment to his native Midwest throughout his literary career. Garland describes his own motives when he says that 'it is the most natural thing in the world for the young writer to love his birthplace, to write of it, to sing of it.' This personal sense of regional loyalty leads Garland to add one important qualification to Howells's definition of local colour: he declares that 'local color ... could not have been written in any other place or by any one else than a native ... The tourist cannot write the local novel' ('Local Color,' 64). Garland's overstated claim is disproved by history (Robert Frost, for example, was a native not of New England, but of California), but it attests to a genuine motive that is integral to regionalism. The difference voiced by Garland introduces an important distinction between Howells's local-colour realism and a more genuine regionalism: it suggests that objective observation and accurate description alone cannot capture regional identity, that regionalism also depends to a certain degree on a 'sense of place' derived through first-hand experience.

The conflicting imperatives of realism and regionalism are evident in Garland's fiction. Although in his nonfiction he seems to have recognized intuitively the limitations of objective observation, despite his protestations to the contrary his fiction succeeds in giving us only an outsider's view of his native Midwest. In a preface to his two-volume collection of short stories set in the Midwest, Garland tells readers that he gathered the material for *Main-traveled Roads* in the summer of 1887. He explains that upon returning to his native Iowa after three years in Boston, 'rural life presented itself from an entirely new angle' (vi). The 'angle' from which Garland was for the first time able to view his region was that of detached, objective observation, and despite brief flashes of lyrical brilliance that attest to a deep personal attachment to the region, that oblique 'angle' prevails: ultimately we are given a picture of the Midwest as seen through the eyes of a tourist.

The protagonist in one of these stories mirrors Garland's own approach to the region. 'Up the Cooly' describes a successful dramatist who returns to his native Wisconsin after living in New York for ten years. As Howard McClane gazes out the window of his westbound train, we are told that the passing scene was '*his* West ... He still took pride in being a Western man' (45). The narrator explains that the local scenery had 'a certain mysterious glamour [for] him; the lakes were cooler and brighter to his eye, the streams fresher, and the grain more golden than to any one else' (45). This introductory scene suggests intriguing possibilities: if the ensuing narration of characters, events, and descriptions were to be filtered through this character's perception, readers might be given insights into a distinct local reality; they might be introduced to a fictional world governed by forces that make '*his* West' different from the West that a tourist on that same train might see. This glimpse of Garland's own regionalist motives, however, is transitory; rather than pursue regional differences accessible only to a native inhabitant, the narrator 'steps back' to situate the story within a broader, homogenizing context.

This context is evident in the story's opening passage, in which readers are introduced to the setting through the protagonist's privileged perspective. As the train approaches McClane's childhood home, the setting first appears as a dot on the horizon; the train then deposits the protagonist in this isolated location before speeding off to rejoin the world that lies beyond the town's horizons: 'He caught sight of the splendid broken line of hills on which his baby eyes had looked thirty-five years ago. A few minutes later, and the train drew up at the grimy little station set into the hillside, and giving him just time to leap off, plunged on again toward the West' (45–46). From the station, Howard looks up at the hills, now a 'majestic amphitheatre ... that circled the horizon' (46). This natural amphitheatre defines the world of the community's inhabitants; ignorant of the world that surrounds their immediate environs, all they see is the 'grimy little station,' the 'squat town' (46), and the poverty of their failed farms. Readers, of course, share the protagonist's privileged view of a single isolated community within the vast American landscape.

While the protagonist of 'Up the Cooly' is able to situate the story's setting within a larger world beyond the region's borders, he is not omniscient; it is left to the narrator to explain the source of the misery that Howard's family is living in. Howard offers his brother money, but the brother refuses, seemingly intuiting that his problem stems from more than a simple lack of money: 'You can't help me now,' he says wearily, 'It's too late' (87). The two characters are left bewildered by the poverty that surrounds them, and the narrator steps in to inform readers that the local squalor is only part of a larger tragedy: 'The struggle for a place to stand on this planet was eating the heart and soul out of men and women in the city, just as in the country' (80). Garland had a very particular idea about the national character that realistic depictions of local environs would reveal: he believed that unfair tax laws encouraged land speculation and were ruining the nation. He was intent on providing in his fiction evidence that would support his active campaign for a single tax ('A New Declaration' 166).

Throughout *Main-traveled Roads*, explanations situating the plight of the region's inhabitants within a broader, unifying context are provided either by an extra-diegetic narrator, or, in highly improbable instances, by characters themselves. In 'Among the Corn Rows,' for example, a grizzled pioneer declares that he had struck out for the western frontier, 'just like a thousand other fellers, to get a start where the cussed European aristocracy hadn't got a holt on the people' (92). In case readers miss the wider implications of this isolated incident, the narrator points out that 'this working farmer had voiced the modern idea. It was an absolute overturn of all the ideas of nobility and special privilege born of the feudal past' (92). Whatever details of local life Garland may present in this story, they are subordinated to this didactic purpose: they symbolize either 'the modern idea' or its antithesis, and are employed in a dramatization of the author's view of the laws responsible for the decay of U.S. society.

Such heavy-handed didacticism is proof that despite his personal attachment to the Midwest Garland's desire to sing the praises of his native region is secondary to his desire to see the region as symptomatic of larger, unifying totalities. Isolated passages in his fiction give glimpses of the regionalist motive he describes in his nonfiction: the description in 'Up the Cooly,' for example, of McClane returning to '*his* West' echoes the personal motive that was missing from Howells's definition; and flashes of brilliant imagery elsewhere suggest insights available only to inhabitants whose lives have been shaped by a very specific sense of place. These passages, however, are ultimately adornments added to fiction whose real subject lies beyond regional borders.

THE MYSTERY OF PLACE: FRANK NORRIS

Whereas Távora's historical realism made use of limited material, regionalists attempting to capture the present as they saw it all around them were faced with a Sisyphean task. Authors who attempted to capture in fiction the identity of the American West at the end of the nineteenth century were faced with particular challenges, which William Everson describes in an essay entitled 'Archetype West.' Everson defines regionalism as 'a quest for the mysterious force that makes a region recognizable as a distinct cultural entity: the mystery of place' (208 n.). He describes that 'mystery of place' in terms of archetype and apotheosis: a region, as Everson sees it, is a pre-existing archetype awaiting a voice, and apotheosis is the intersection of the mystery of place with the voice of creative genius. According to Everson's theory, whereas East Coast society evolved around a vertical social hierarchy, western society was more horizontal, less structured, and to capture this horizontal social landscape in fiction would require 'eruptive intensity of energy, monumental output, overwhelming pantheistic vision' (254).

It would be hard to find anywhere a more apt description of the regionalist project undertaken by Frank Norris in his novel *The Octopus*. Subtitled 'A Story of California,' it is a massive volume of realistic fiction devoted to capturing the West as Norris saw it at the close of the century. *The Octopus* is the second of three novels in Norris's short literary career (he died at the age of thirty-two) that bear titles attesting to regionalist intentions: chronologically, it falls between *McTeague: A Story of San Francisco* and *The Pit: A Story of Chicago*. *McTeague* is a slender volume, and, despite its subtitle, its most valuable contribution to regionalist art is not its rendition of San Francisco, but its brilliant evocation of Death Valley in the latter third of the novel. After expanding his regionalist project with *The Octopus*, Norris effectively abandons regionalism altogether in *The Pit*, a novel in which specificity of place plays no part whatsoever (the commodities market around which the central plot turns happens to be located in Chicago).

A clue to Norris's straying from his regionalist intentions late in his career can be found in his depiction in *The Octopus* of a minor character who is intent on composing a regionalist poem. The character expresses regionalist motives similar to Norris's own, and he employs realist methods duplicating those evident in Norris's own novel; yet the fictional author's regionalist project is a dismal failure. In one brief scene in particular, in which Presley sits down to compose his regionalist epic, Norris seems to confront directly the futility of his own methods; yet lacking an alternative, he perseveres with his story of California, and goes on to pursue a lifetime regionalist project that would become increasingly distant from his original regionalist motives.

Through Presley, Norris expands on the regionalist motives he and
Garland had both hinted at in their critical essays. We are told that
Presley 'strove for the diapason, the great song that should embrace in
itself ... the voice of an entire people' (9). The fictional author envisions
this 'diapason' as a massive catalogue of local details, and as he considers
everything that would have to go into this 'Song of the West,' the project
takes on monumental proportions. His poem will have to include the
people who inhabit the region and everything that makes them distinct
from people elsewhere, including 'their legends, their folklore, their
fightings, their loves and their lusts, their blunt, grim humour, their
stoicism under stress, their adventures, their treasures found in a day and
gambled in a night, their direct rude speech, their generosity and cruelty,
their heroicism and bestiality, their religion and profanity, their self-
sacrifice and obscenity (10). Presley's epic poem will also have to include
all the distinctive characteristics of the region's geography: not only the
canyons and mesas, but also 'the valley, the plain, and the mountain; the
ranch, the range, and the mine' (10). Presley's goal is to see all these
details of people and place 'gathered together, swept together, welded
and riven together in one single mighty song, the Song of the West' (10).

Throughout the novel, Presley struggles to gather the material for this
regionalist project. He crisscrosses the region by foot, by horse, and on
bicycle, noting all the pertinent details. He climbs hilltops to gaze at the
region, and at one point as he gazes at the landscape below him, he
believes he has come close to grasping the material of his great song:
'Ha! there it was, his epic, his inspiration, his West, his thundering progression of hexameters. A sudden uplift, a sense of exhilaration, of
physical exaltation appeared abruptly to sweep Presley from his feet. As
from a point high above the world, he seemed to dominate a universe,
a whole order of things. He was dizzied, stunned, stupefied' (47). When
Presley later sits at his desk to compose his poem, he recalls the view
from atop the hill, and 'the details came thronging back – the compo-
nent parts of his poem, the signs and symbols of the West' (47). These
details, however, stubbornly resist being 'riven' together in an ordered
progression of 'thundering hexameters.' When he takes up his pen, the
images dissolve and 'things without names – thoughts for which no man
had yet invented words, terrible formless shapes, vague figures, colossal,
monstrous, distorted – whirled at a gallop through his imagination' (10).
Presley is discouraged, but does not immediately abandon hope: 'But the
stuff is *here*,' he mutters to himself, 'I'll get hold of it yet' (13).

The closer Presley comes to grasping those elusive images, the closer he comes to crossing an ontological border by taking the place of the actual author. He comes precipitously close to crossing that border when he abandons poetry and transfers his regionalist project to prose. When several pages of the resulting journal are transcribed directly in Norris's novel, the crossing is almost complete; the journal threatens to become the novel we are reading, and the character is close to becoming his own creator. Such ontological border-crossings, however, are forbidden by the poetics of realism, and Presley's journal remains safely contained within the frame of the novel's fictional world; he eventually finds prose no more conducive to his task than poetry and finally abandons his 'song' altogether, contenting himself instead with a short poem entitled 'The Toiler' (inspired by a Millet painting), which describes the exploitation of workers by the railroad.

Having failed to capture the West in song, Presley becomes just another element in the list of ingredients that would be included in Norris's own vision of the West. Constrained by the borders of the novel's fictional world, Presley is incapable of achieving the distance that realist authors saw as essential to capturing regional identity. The novel's narrator shares no such restriction, however, and it is from the narrator's extra-diegetic perspective that the West is finally framed within the pages of *The Octopus*.

Presley's frustration is portrayed as due partly to geographic limitations – it seems at times that if he could only find a hilltop high enough he could grasp the image he is seeking. When Presley leaves the region altogether at the end of the novel, however, he confronts a limitation of another kind. Climbing another hill for one last look at the region before his departure, for the first time he faces questions that transgress the limits of his regional study; he 'seemed for an instant to touch the explanation of existence' (634). But the revelation is transitory; the 'instant' vanishes, and as the region fades to a dot on the horizon beyond the departing freighter, the bewildered character is left asking himself, 'What was the full round of the circle whose segment only he beheld?' (651). Presley's failed regionalism is thus attributed not only to ontological limitations, but also to a kind of epistemological shortsightedness – an inability to understand forces emanating from beyond the region's borders.

Through the novel's narrator, Norris provides the knowledge that the character lacks. The 'whole order of things' that had eluded Presley is finally revealed when the narrator informs us that the novel's characters are mere 'motes in the sunshine' (651), pawns governed by universal forces: 'The Wheat is one force, the Railroad, another, and there is the law that governs them – supply and demand' (576). The bewildering matrix of people and place that Presley had confronted is ordered in a drama that is played out on a global stage; *The Octopus* is finally not a 'story of California' at all, but a story of universal forces represented by the wheat and the railroad. The homogenizing context that Howells found in a smiling portrait of America, and that Garland found in unjust tax laws, is for Norris manifest in determinist economic and natural laws.

The kind of 'difference' that Garland advocated is illustrated on two levels in *The Octopus*. On a thematic level, the novel contains an abundance of distinctive local detail: from barn-dance romances to saloon shoot-outs, all the images that have become the stock-in-trade of Western fiction are included in Norris's novel. On the level of narration, the novel's framing technique demonstrates how ontological borders might be manipulated to portray regional difference. Characters groping for the 'full round,' and struggling to comprehend the unnameable force that rules their lives, come close to transgressing the sacrosanct borders of realism's one-world ontology. The overseeing narrator, however, frames these gropings for an unnameable other within a homogenizing context: the knowable universe from which Norris, like Cunha and Távora, launched his investigation of regional identity.

William Everson is reluctant to classify *The Octopus* as an example of the kind of apotheosis that he describes; the novel could, however, be considered an apotheosis of another kind – not of one region's identity, but of realist regionalism. Its massive catalogue of local details tests the limits of what Henry James had described as the 'capacious vessel' of realist fiction.[5] Although the novel's thematic testing of borders comes close to undermining realism's monolithic ontology, its strictly hierarchical framework ultimately serves to fortify those borders. The external perspective of the novel's narrator enables the demarcation of succinct borders, isolating the region for scrutiny. Rather than focus on the 'substance,' 'the mystery of place,' or the 'mysterious catalytic force' that accounts for regional difference, though, in the end the novel subordinates this difference to universal laws that transcend regional borders.

CONCLUSION

The political influences on Brazilian literature that Cândido and Süssekind describe resulted in some significant differences between Brazilian and United States regionalism. Regionalism and politics had been inseparable throughout nineteenth-century Brazil, from Magalhães's dream of national autonomy to Távora and Cunha's explicit demands for a reversal of Brazil's centralist sociopolitical structure. The influence of politics on U.S. regionalism was more benign: Cooper was more interested in cultural unity than in political autonomy, and although Norris hints at political connections between the railroad and East Coast powers, his concern with deterministic laws of man and nature overshadow any concern for the marginalizing influences of national politics.

Nevertheless, significant similarities between the North Americans Garland and Norris, on the one hand, and the Brazilians Távora and Cunha on the other indicate some common influences spanning the two hemispheres. All of the novels we have looked at in this chapter illustrate a separation of subject and object that seeks to empower literature with the truth claim of the natural sciences. The new-found authority of detached observation led Cunha to view the Canudos rebellion as a 'chapter in the history of the Earth' (295), and Norris to view the subject of his novel as a 'passing phase of history' (*Octopus* 10). The reduction of history to a succession of frozen moments is common to realism in general; in regionalism, however, this narrative authority not only led to heightened specificity of time, but provided a means of isolating specificity of place. The added influence of positivism provided a means of attempting to quantify the effect of this specificity of time and place on human identity. The mystery of place that had been a vague intuition to romantic authors was now subject to rigorous empirical scrutiny.

Realism introduced the importance of regional difference by emphasizing the geographic borders that isolate a region from the world around it. Although this all-important recognition of difference led to increased awareness of specificity of time and place, the realist perception of difference is merely a transposition of values in the romantic self/other dialectic. Whether a region is viewed from within, by one looking outward to distant horizons, or from the external perspective of a distant observer, the result is the same: a yearning for belonging and homogeneity. The romantic yearning for cultural homogeneity is merely replaced by a realist desire to frame regions in a homogeneous, one-world ontology.

Regionalism flourished under the poetics of realism. The common-sense perception of a region as a natural object was never questioned; authors had only to be astute observers and books to be capacious vessels, and the mystery of place would be solved. Definitions of regionalism formulated at that time are for the most part the definitions that remain with us today. Realist authors with a gift for observation and a talent for storytelling have given regionalism a limited degree of legitimacy in contemporary criticism, but regionalism, insofar as it is recognized at all, survives only as an anachronism. Talented realists can be entertaining and enlightening, but portraits of regions as static tableaux in a 'passing phase of history' do not convey the dynamic interplay of forces along regional borders that is the source of a vital regional identity.

Although few critics have seriously considered regionalism as worthy of re-examination in light of post-realist poetics, a few isolated twentieth-century authors have experimented with non-realist alternatives to traditional notions of regionalism. Regionalist works that defy such realist conventions as omniscient narration, third-person narration, past-tense narration, and unity of plot and character have been either neglected by publishers and critics, or accepted for reasons other than their depiction of a specific place and its effect on human identity. Regionalists are likely to be tolerated only if one accepts such qualifications as that expressed by the Canadian author W.O. Mitchell, who apologizes for his own regionalism by explaining that he 'can't go to work on a piece unless I have some essentially human truth that I believe very passionately and that I hope shall transcend time and region' (54). Some twentieth-century authors whose literary careers were dominated by a compulsion to capture the mystery of place have even been canonized, but at the expense of denying their regionalism. Faulkner, for example, is recognized as a master at depicting the American South, but always with the qualification that he also exemplifies something less restricted by time and place – human psychology, for instance, or modernist poetics. It can be argued, however, that Faulkner and other non-realist regionalists are motivated first and foremost by a desire to capture the 'mysterious force' that lies behind regional identity, and that insights into the human condition are a fortunate by-product of this regional investigation.

Although regional borders are partly defined by such natural phenomena as temperature, elevation, and rainfall, and even by such quantifiable human phenomena as speech and customs, simply quantifying these data will not uncover the mystery of regional identity. Regionalism stems from a personal sense of place, and therein lies the intentionality of regionalist fiction. Denying that intentionality will result in a static portrait that succeeds only in covering up difference. The twentieth century brought more than one alternative to realism, and each would present innovative means of investigating regional difference. The early decades of the century were marked by a radical rejection of realist poetics, and, as we shall see in the next chapter, the alternatives offered by modernism resulted in a new approach to investigating the mystery of place.

CHAPTER THREE

Inside Out

MODERNIST POETICS AND REGIONAL DIFFERENCE

Critics continue to debate whether early twentieth-century innovators in the arts represent a decisive break in a centuries-old humanist tradition or merely represent a resurgence of earlier trends towards aestheticism. Regardless of its implications for art theory, though, and despite its diverse manifestations, the term 'modernism' designates a body of early twentieth-century works of art that make a clear departure from those of previous generations. Malcolm Bradbury describes this departure when he refers to works that 'no longer appear to witness to the same kind of consciousness, nor to refer to the same type of historical experience, nor to relate to the same processes of imagining, nominalizing, or alluding to exterior life as they did before' (312). These works are characterized by a heightened attention to the cognitive processes of human perception and a foregrounding of aesthetic form. This heightened subjectivity and aestheticism led to the common perception of modernism as a kind of escapism, according to one definition, 'the recoil of the individual from a hostile world into private codes' (Hoffman et al. 21).

For regionalists adopting modernist techniques, modernism entailed a conflation of regional borders with the epistemological borders that define individual identity. Rather than view a region from afar as the 'segment only' of a 'full round,' as Norris ultimately does in *The Octopus*, the modernist author viewed the region from within, and portrayed it as an autonomous world whose borders are under constant threat from external forces. In regionalist fiction the sense of alienation that is common in modernist art becomes politicized: typically the author portrays a region as the victim of an unjust centralized society.

Modernist regionalism was far more popular in Latin America than in North America: many of the avant-garde movements that sprang up throughout the southern Americas in the 1920s and 1930s adopted local environments as their subject matter. More cosmopolitan avant-garde movements, however, derided that regionalism as provincial, and heated rivalries arose between the more Eurocentric avant-garde movements and their regionalist counterparts.[1] In this chapter I will focus on a modernist regionalist movement in northeastern Brazil that is typical of such movements throughout Latin America, and on one isolated regionalist work from Mexico that brings into sharp relief modernist regionalism's affinity with post-colonialism.

Regionalism was less popular in the United States and Canada in the twenties and thirties, but in chapter 4 we will see examples of a regionalist movement in the southern United States that bears striking similarities to its Latin American counterparts, and of isolated authors in Western Canada who adapted modernist poetics to their regionalist fiction.

BRAZIL: THE NORTHEAST NOVELS OF THE 1930S

Regionalism had played a prominent role in nineteenth-century Brazilian literature. From José de Alencar's declaration that only in the unspoiled backlands 'can be found in its original purity ... the singular being of our country,' (Sonhos, cited by J.M. Almeida 37), to Franklin Távora's theory that the rural Northeast could provide 'the elements for the creation of a uniquely Brazilian literature, born of the earth' (Távora, cited by Castello iv), authors were determined to describe Brazil's exotic geography in an attempt to capture the essence of Brazilian identity. These authors succeeded, however, only in propagating European values: Alencar's romantic indigenism embodied European ideals by depicting Indians as 'noble savages,' and Távora's realism reinforced European dominance by depicting the poverty and backwardness of the New World.

The beginning of the twentieth century saw a growing scepticism among Brazilian critics, a sense that formerly unquestioned epistemological assumptions – assumptions concerning the relationship between self and world, and even the relationship between Brazilians and Western civilization – were unsuited to the investigation of the unique Brazilian identity that authors sought. An early twentieth-century critic, José Verissimo, described a widespread disillusionment with a literature that applied European methods to an indigenous Brazilian reality: 'There has always been too much literature in this literature, and it was always made, albeit with profound sympathy, with a European mentality, with a European sentiment, with European aesthetics, processes, modes, and literary mannerisms. The intimate, congenial correlation between the artist and his material, from which sincere and creative inspiration must proceed, is not common in our literature' (85).

Verissimo did not see among the works of his contemporaries an alternative to the nineteenth-century art form he criticized, but the generally felt discontent he expressed continued to grow, until, in February 1922, it gave rise to a series of readings, performances, and exhibitions in São Paulo that came to be known as the Week of Modern Art. The São Paulo modernists broke with tradition by introducing political urgency to art, by departing from nineteenth-century concepts of mimetic illusion, and by introducing a new focus on the act of artistic creation as an end in itself.

The Week of Modern Art spawned many attempts to fuse stylistic innovation with indigenous materials, most notably the short-lived Antropofagía movement, spearheaded by Mario de Andrade. The movement's name (literally, 'cannibalism') is a satirical reference to European stereotypes of New World natives: Andrade called for a return to 'head-hunting,' advocating a literature that would 'devour' its European predecessors ('De antropofagía'). Despite the satiric reference to cannibalism, Andrade's intentions were earnest: he advocated an indigenism that by its very outrageousness would destroy the stereotypes propagated by the more traditional indigenism of authors like Alencar. The lasting monument of the movement is Andrade's *Macunaíma*, a brief tale of a native Tupí Indian that is so densely packed with indigenous vocabulary and fragments of indigenous folklore as to be inaccessible to all but the expert anthropologist.

A group of Northeast writers, led by the sociologist Gilberto Freyre, resented the São Paulo modernists' claims to be speaking for all Brazilians, in particular the claim of the Antropofagía movement to be representing a genuine indigenous culture. The Northeasterners protested that São Paulo modernism was nothing more than an eclectic grab-bag of Brazilian themes defaced by abstract aesthetic values borrowed from Europe, and that the São Paulo artists did nothing to promote a distinct Brazilian cultural identity. As well as responding to the São Paulo modernists, the Northeasterners were addressing renewed social and political threats to their regional identity. The abolition of slavery in 1888 had upset the agrarian economy of the Northeast, and a series of military coups resulted in an increasingly centralist government based in the South. The republican constitution of 1889 was first challenged by the military in 1922; when the army finally took power in 1930, the military dictatorship of Getúlio Dórtico Vargas would promote centralized modernization as the antidote to Brazil's backwardness.

The Northeast regionalist movement began with Freyre's return to his native Recife after years of study in Europe and the United States. Intrigued by the wealth of cultural material he found in the Brazilian northeast, Freyre undertook what he termed a 'pesquisa regionalista' (regionalist investigation), which culminated in his organization of the 1926 Primeiro Congreso Brasileiro do Regionalismo (First Brazilian Regionalist Conference). Freyre's conference emphasized cuisine and folk art more than literature, but the regionalist movement it initiated was responsible for a boom in literary production that has been canonized in Brazilian literature as 'the Northeast novel of the 'thirties.'[2] Among the novelists who acknowledge Freyre's influence are some of the most prominent in twentieth-century Brazilian literature, including José Américo de Almeida, Rachel de Queiroz, Graciliano Ramos, José Lins do Rêgo, and Jorge Amado.

Although Freyre was intent on distancing his regionalist movement from the São Paulo modernists,[3] their break from tradition and their formal experimentation undoubtedly contributed to the possibility of a new approach to regionalist literature. Nevertheless, Freyre explains that for the Northeast authors aesthetic experimentation never overshadowed the authors' personal 'feel' for the region: 'With these "innovators" the *regional* was never separated from the *human*; nor was for any of them the desire for literary, artistic, sociological or psychological experimentation greater than their feel for the living subject' (*Região e tradição* 55). Freyre's attention to the immediate experience of regionalism responds to Verissimo's call for an 'intimate, congenial correlation between the artist and his material' by infusing modernist innovation with the personal sense of place that is the starting point of all regionalism.

The Northeast movement of the 1930s responded in a variety of ways to the converging forces of politics, poetics, and regionalism. José Américo de Almeida's *A bagaceira* was the first novel to come out of the movement, and its contribution lies mainly in its break from tradition through its thematic depiction of regional backwardness. Graciliano Ramos's *Vidas sêcas* demonstrates how traditional narrative structure can be manipulated to reflect the distinct rhythms underlying the daily lives of the region's inhabitants, and José Lins do Rêgo's *Fogo morto* combines thematic sociopolitical conflicts with even more radical stylistic experimentation.

A BAGACEIRA

A bagaceira conforms to the traditional definition of regionalism as fiction that portrays a particular place and the effect of that place on its inhabitants, but the effect of place on people in *A bagaceira* does not involve a passive absorption of environmental traits. The novel depicts the region as being in violent conflict with a threatening external world, and it is this conflict that shapes the lives of the novel's characters. On a thematic level, regional and personal identities are threatened by external forces, and on an epistemic and ontological level, internal worlds are threatened with extinction.

A bagaceira's most obvious break from nineteenth-century tradition is its explicit criticism of the utopian visions offered by both Alencar's primitivism and Távora's 'emporiums of commerce.' Almeida's novel does include some idyllic descriptions of the Northeast: depictions of a 'green forest [that] glowed in an orgy of golden blossom' (17), for example, and of 'the clamorous joy of tropical nature' (25) are reminiscent of Alencar's 'virgin ground,' or Távora's 'fantastic temple.' These idyllic visions, however, are rare; much more common are portrayals of filth and decay. The fictional world of Távora's *O cabeleira* would not have accommodated such scenes as the following: 'She felt nauseated when they visited their miserable hovels with the floor stinking of stale urine and pestilence, and the scrofulous children, covered in boils, forever scratching their diseased skins. Pot-bellied, with legs like sticks, they looked like oranges stuck with a couple of tooth-picks; their hair, grey with lice, stank of bad eggs' (93).

As in previous regionalist novels, the Northeast's natural environment is portrayed as emblematic of the Brazilian spirit, but in *A bagaceira* this wild spirit is revealed to have a dark, violent side. In one shocking passage, the narrator describes in graphic detail how a young woman is raped while bathing beneath a waterfall, and presents the violent scene as symptomatic of Brazil's savage nature. The passage begins with a typically romantic homage to natural beauty, including descriptions of cascading water that 'seemed to smother [the young woman] in pearls,' and of 'brazen little puddles from which the sun gazed up at her nudity,' together with reference to the 'naked freedom' with which 'her rounded figure displayed itself' (141–2). The scene quickly turns ugly, however, as the woman realizes that the plantation owner is spying on her, and she flees through a dense tangle of thorns, only to be overtaken and raped. The passage's conclusion offers a striking contrast to earlier romantic depictions of the region: 'There was nothing here of nymphs or fawns, just stark, primitive urges – primeval Brazil, with naked women in the woods' (141–2).

The 'woods' in *A bagaceira* are far from the edenic world that had provided a mythical backdrop for Alencar: they are violent and threatening: 'The wild jungle appeared to him a conflict: trees crushing down other trees; deformities like those of human beings; hunchbacked plants bent to the ground, venerable trunks strangled by creepers' (22). Not only is this descriptive passage anti-romantic in content, it also suggests a deeply rooted criticism of the homogeneous ontology of nineteenth-century regionalism. The passage concludes with Lúcio, the protagonist, 'afraid that the insidious creepers would entangle his aching body in their dangling coils and imprison him in this hostile solitude' (22). In this description, the same jungle that had, in the previous century, been a temple ensuring Brazil's rightful place in God's creation is portrayed as a prison isolating its inhabitants from the outside world.

While such descriptions in themselves were sufficiently shocking at the time of its publication, break with tradition extends beyond a thematic treatment of the landscape. An epistemic shift is apparent in the first sentence of the novel: *A bagaceira* opens with a narrowly focalized perspective unlike *O sertanejo*'s nonfocalized perspective of an 'immense plain' stretching towards 'infinite horizons'[4]: 'With lunch over – it was around nine o'clock – as if impelled by some intense curiosity, Dagoberto Marçau posted himself at the window, which is one way of escaping from the house without going out of doors' (13). The character gazing out a window is emblematic of a new approach to regionalism: Almeida portrays self and region as united behind epistemological and ontological barriers that define an autonomous, internal world divorced from a disordered and threatening external world. Almeida also draws a parallel between borders that define personal identity and regional identity and borders that separate fictional worlds from the real world of author and reader.

Lúcio, the novel's protagonist, is engaged in an endless conflict between the claustrophobic world of his own thoughts and the exterior world of his surroundings. This conflict is dramatized in an early scene in which Lúcio locks himself in his room, 'as if making himself his own prisoner' (24). After a period of introspection during which he remembers his childhood as a 'world of closed doors,' he gets up and scribbles his thoughts on the wall: 'I cried in the morning as the birds began to sing ... Milonga would say, "The bogeyman's on his way killing little boys ...," and I would curl up, making myself so tiny that the world won't see me ... Today I can't make myself so tiny that the world won't see me' (24). The transmigration of this mini-narrative from the character's thoughts to the bedroom wall suggests the crossing of an ontological border, from the internal world of thought to the external world of physical presence. The wall itself suggests another border, containing thought and narration within the internal space of the house.

Throughout *A bagaceira* we are reminded of borders that define isolated, internal worlds. In one scene, Lúcio retires to a grove of cashew trees and within this 'natural bower' retreats to the private world of romantic novels: 'Instead of communing with the classical "Book of Nature," he spurned these green leaves with their multicolored illustrations to immerse himself in degenerate romanticism' (41). In another scene, a long first-person narration of a lifetime spent fleeing the Northeast's periodic droughts is enclosed in the interior of a character's hut. The passage begins by situating the hut against 'a vast sunset' that 'lit up half the sky' (45), but as the embedded narrative begins the focalization switches to the hut's interior. Part way through, Valentim's narration is interrupted when Lúcio gets up to gaze out the door, and readers get a view from the inside looking out when Lúcio comments to Valentim, 'It's as black as pitch outside.' Valentim responds by asking, 'Are you feeling the cold?' and then, after taking a pinch of snuff, he resumes his narration (47). The imagery reflects the internal focalization that predominates in the novel: the hut that contains the narrative is a pinpoint of light set against an impenetrable void.

The embedded narration mirrors the novel's central theme of isolation: just as Lúcio's childhood world is strictly circumscribed by his immediate surroundings, from within Valentim's hut nothing exists beyond its walls but a cold, black void. The region's isolation is broken as the novel progresses, when Lúcio crosses its geographic boundaries to attend university. When he returns, he brings with him the latest technology from the outside world and proceeds to transform his plantation into a model of modern efficiency. In modernizing the plantation, Lúcio flattens the natural features that had distinguished the region, and this sets off a chain reaction that results in the annihilation of regional identity. The workers become so alienated from the land that 'to them geography was a mere notion of vagabondage; hygiene, a hatred of the unclean soil'

(158). Individual alienation leads to the loss of a collective cultural identity, as is evident at a local celebration: 'The laughter-loving people of the barbaric sambas had changed: the popular dances had been abolished and the staid waltzes were as if weighed down by elephantiasis' (157).

The thematic content of *A bagaceira* shows how regionalism can derive substance from more than just colourful description. *A bagaceira* is a coming-of-age novel, with the protagonist's loss of innocence tied directly to a conflict between region and world. The young Lúcio's introspection is paralleled by the region's isolation from the outside world; Lúcio's journey outside of his introspective isolation and into the external world is paralleled by the annihilation of borders separating region from world. Both cases involve a conflict between interior and exterior worlds, but the homogeneous ontology underlying realist poetics is nevertheless triumphant: with the demolition of borders separating self from world, autonomous identity   both of self and of region – is consumed by the exterior world.

A bagaceira's conclusion reveals an ambivalent attitude towards regionalism. In contrast to nineteenth-century visions of an integration of region and world – such as Alencar's assimilation of primitive backlanders with heroic myth, or Távora's integration of nature's 'fantastic temple' with the 'economic emporiums' of modern commerce (13) – Almeida's vision is of region and world in fundamental opposition. The novel's conclusion suggests that modern industrialization is both desirable and inevitable, yet laments the resulting loss of autonomous regional identity.

Almeida's breakthrough was to recognize identity as difference. His novel does not attempt to assimilate regional identity with universal values, but presents the differences that define a distinct regional world from within that world. Although *A bagaceira* achieves a thematic foregrounding of difference, the continuing pull of the conventions of realism prevents the novel from doing more than describing regional difference from a distance and portraying the collapse of regional borders as inevitable. The abandonment of realism's external perspective would entail crossing over to the internal space of modernist fiction; *A bagaceira* approaches that internal space and holds it up for examination, but ultimately fails to secure that internal world against the homogeneous space in which realist fiction is anchored. The Northeast novelists that followed *A bagaceira*'s example would further exploit the correlation between aesthetic autonomy and regional difference.

VIDAS SÊCAS

Graciliano Ramos's *Vidas sêcas* portrays a conflict between region and world similar to that in *A bagaceira*, but the novel's narration is focalized even more predominantly from within the region and its conflict is not resolved. By disrupting the linear plot of traditional narrative in order to present the seasonal cycles of the northeast *sertão*, Ramos creates a fictional world defined entirely by regional forces. The novel offers neither an idealistic vision of evolutionary progress nor a determinist vision of the region's inevitable collapse; instead it portrays the Northeast's isolation and poverty, and its domination by sophisticated outsiders as a perpetual condition resulting from the region's harsh climate and topography.

Some readers have criticized *Vidas sêcas* for its lack of narrative coherence and have called the work a collection of independent short stories rather than a novel.[5] *Vidas sêcas* has no discernible plot: it begins and ends with a family wandering the *sertão* in search of refuge from the drought, and there is no causal connection between events that occur in the intervening chapters. One critic, however, argues that the novel employs a different kind of textual coherence: not only do the scenes repeated in the first and last chapters frame the entire novel within the drought cycle of the *sertão*, but the intervening chapters echo this symmetrical repetition, framing the narrated characters and events within a perpetual movement from drought to flood and back to drought.[6] The novel's thirteen chapters can be seen as a concentric series of six frames, at the centre of which is chapter 7, which describes the family gathered around their fire as the river swells under the downpour. At the furthest remove from this centre are chapters 2 and 12, in which Fabiano, the father and husband in this family of wandering *sertanejos*, contemplates first his success at finding a refuge during the flood (in chapter 2), and then his impending departure from that refuge (in chapter 12). Moving inward towards the central chapter, the next frame is provided by chapters 3 and 11, both of which describe Fabiano's exploitation by a policeman. Chapters 4 and 10 describe the landowner's exploitation of the family; chapters 5 and 9 describe the blind obedience paid to Fabiano from his younger son's perspective (chapter 5) and from the dog's perspective (chapter 9); and in chapters 6 and 8, the characters ponder some of the incomprehensible, unattainable worlds that lie beyond the existence that they know (the green hills beyond the *sertão* in chapter 6, and the chaos of the city in chapter 8).

Within each chapter the cyclical life of the *sertanejo* is reflected in narrative segments that 'go' nowhere. In chapter 11, for example, Fabiano encounters a policeman in the woods; his first impulse is to strike the policeman with his machete, but he arrests the impulse. The policeman asks for directions, and Fabiano shows him the way. The physical encounter is over in a matter of seconds, yet its narration fills six pages, describing in detail the sluggish thoughts of the *sertanejo* in response to an emissary of external authority. The episode begins on page 102, when Fabiano comes face to face with the policeman and, acting on his first impulse, raises his machete: 'the impulse lasted only a second, no, a fraction of a second.' Five pages later Fabiano reflects that 'if things had lasted a second longer, the policeman would be dead,' but in these five pages 'things' have barely progressed beyond that first fraction of a second. At the end of the chapter the narrated action resumes when Fabiano drops his machete: 'He drew back, perturbed. Seeing him thus humble and orderly, the policeman pricked up courage and advanced, stepping firmly, to ask directions. Fabiano took off his leather hat, bowed, and showed him the way' (108).

The exaggerated internal focalization that predominates in this chapter – as in most of the novel – creates a narrowly circumscribed fictional world. In this instance, by limiting the narration to the severely restricted world of Fabiano's thoughts, Ramos portrays an intrusion from the outside world as entirely foreign and incomprehensible. This passage demonstrates a reversal of the perspective on regional marginality that had previously prevailed in Northeast regionalism. Unlike Távora's account of the misunderstood *cangaceiro* or Cunha's depiction of the persecuted mystic, Ramos portrays the region's marginal existence not from the external perspective of a moralizing narrator, but from the internal perspective of the *sertanejo*.

Ramos also uses language to link the region to the lives of its inhabitants and to emphasize the alienation of the region from the external world. In his daily interactions with his immediate environs Fabiano has little use for the language of civilized society: 'He marvelled at the long, difficult words used by town folk, and sought vainly to repeat some of them, though he knew they were useless and perhaps dangerous' (16–17). When one of his sons approaches Fabiano with a question, he is at first perplexed, and then annoyed. He ignores the boy's attempt at conversation and reflects that if it weren't for the endless cycle of drought and flood, there might be a place for language in the life of the *sertanejo*: 'Some day – Yes, when droughts went away and everything was right – ... Free of that danger the boys could talk, ask questions, and do anything they liked. But now they had to behave like the kind of people they were' (21–2).

Fabiano's wife, Vitória, is the only family member who approaches linguistic fluency, and through language she attains a momentary escape from the narrow confines of her immediate world. As the family wanders the *sertão* Vitória is overcome by an acute sense of loneliness, which she seeks to alleviate through language: 'Vitória simply had to talk. If she kept silent she would be like a cactus plant, drying up and dying. She wanted to deceive herself, to cry out that she was strong and that all this – the frightful heat, the trees that were no more than twisted branches, the motionlessness and silence of the range – meant nothing' (123). Vitória's dream that linguistic fluency would deliver her from the solitude of the *sertão* is indeed a deception: throughout *Vidas sêcas* communication is invariably thwarted and characters are condemned to lives as solitary and unchanging as that of the cactus that characterizes the region's flora. Even when Fabiano and Vitória attempt to converse while the family is gathered around the fire during the flood, they lack the necessary linguistic tools and remain isolated: 'It wasn't really a conversation, just a series of isolated phrases, marked by repetitions and incongruities. Sometimes a guttural interjection lent force to a sentence of ambiguous meaning. The fact was that neither of the parents was paying any attention to the words of the other' (64).

When Fabiano and his family travel into the local town, their linguistic ignorance denies them access to the foreign world of urban society. The two boys remain isolated from a world to which they are unable to attach appropriate words:

Then a new problem presented itself to his mind and he whispered it in his brother's ear: In all probability those things had names. The younger boy looked at him questioningly. Yes, surely all the precious things exhibited on the altars and on the shelves in the stores had names.

They began to discuss the perplexing question. How could men keep so many words in their heads? It was impossible; no one could have so vast a store of knowledge. Free of names, things seemed distant and mysterious. (84)

Fabiano's inability to formulate a sentence even denies him the possibility of picking a fight with the villagers. He searches in vain for an insult to hurl at passersby: ' "Pack of –" He stopped in an agony of cold sweat, his mouth full of saliva, unable to find the right word' (79). He paces back and forth in confusion, until, on the following page, the word finally comes to him:

'He gave a harsh cry and slapped his hands together. "A pack of dogs!"'
(80). By now, however, his rage has been succeeded by befuddlement, and
town folk pass him by, oblivious to his ranting.

Their pre-linguistic ignorance explains not only the *sertanejos'* isolation,
but also their exploitation at the hands of the political and economic
powers that reside in the foreign world of urban society. When Fabiano
settles his account at the end of a season's work and comes away owing
the landowner money, he is given the simple explanation that 'the
difference represented interest' (94). The word is incomprehensible to
Fabiano, but he is defenceless against the language of the bosses:

Whenever men with book learning used big words in dealing with him, he came
out the loser. It startled him just to hear those words. Obviously they were just a
cover for robbery.

But they sounded nice. Sometimes he memorized a few of them and introduced them into the conversation at the wrong moment. Then he forgot them
... In difficult moments he would stammer and get all mixed up like a little boy;
he would scratch his elbows in vexation. This was why they skinned him, the
scoundrels! They would take from a poor devil that didn't have a cent to his
name. (98–9)

Fabiano's linguistic incompetence is also responsible for his abuse at
the hands of the town's justice system. When he is assaulted by a policeman, Fabiano protests, and the next thing he knows he is standing before
a judge, where he 'listened without understanding to a charge made
against him, and offered no defense' (27). Beaten and thrown in jail,
Fabiano lets out a cry of rage, and a jailer approaches, telling him to
settle down, that nothing is the matter. 'But a lot of things were the
matter,' Fabiano reflects, 'he just couldn't explain them' (27).

The pre-linguistic ignorance of Ramos's characters is hardly the celebration of natural piety that Alencar attributed to the 'wild song' of
isolated regions. Ramos uses his characters' backwardness to reiterate a
theme that Távora had voiced: that the imbalance of power in Brazil was
responsible for the continued poverty and misery of the Northeast. But
by portraying the region's alienation from an internal perspective, Ramos
also links that poverty and backwardness to internal causes, to the region's harsh climate and barren topography. Fabiano's vision of the day
'when droughts went away and everything was right' offers little hope of
redressing the conditions responsible for the the region's isolation.
Távora's optimistic vision of a realignment of political and economic

powers is replaced in *Vidas sêcas* by a stoic resignation to the conditions inherent in the regional climate and topography.

Ramos draws on his own first-hand experience of life in the *sertão* to place the region in a fictional world that is not framed from an external perspective. The outside world intrudes thematically in the form of the policeman, and of the villagers, who speak a language that is incomprehensible to the *sertanejo*, but the novel portrays these as fragmentary intrusions from a world ordered by a linear temporality and by linguistic patterns alien to the *sertanejo*. In *Vidas sêcas* Ramos undertakes the difficult task of portraying the external world as alien, while employing the very language that alienates the region in the novel's third-person narration.

The disruption of the linear syntax of traditional plot is only a partial step towards the undermining of traditional narrative forms in order to portray regional difference. A more radical disruption of narrative and linguistic convention can be seen in José Lins do Rêgo's *Fogo morto*, which, published in 1945, was the last novel to emanate from the regionalist movement initiated by Freyre.

FOGO MORTO

José Lins do Rêgo was Freyre's most devoted follower among the Northeast regionalist authors.[7] Prompted by Freyre, Lins do Rêgo inaugurated his literary career by publishing three realistic novels chronicling plantation life in the Northeast. Following another series of novels, devoted to regional themes such as mysticism and banditry, in 1943 – almost twenty years after Freyre's First Brazilian Regional Conference – Lins do Rêgo returned to the plantation theme with his novel *Fogo morto*. The Santa Fe plantation on which *Fogo morto* is set is a self-contained agrarian patriarchy of the kind described by Freyre in such sociological studies as *Casa-Grande e Senezala* (The Big House and the Shack) and *Sobrados e Mucambos* (Mansions and Shanties). The Santa Fe of Lins do Rêgo's novel was founded by Captain Tomás, a fiercely independent pioneer, and was handed down to Luís de Holanda, nicknamed Lula by local residents (the nickname is a satire of gentrified farmers and, translated literally, means 'squid from Holland'). Lula becomes the sole male descendant by marrying Tomás's daughter, and thus the region is portrayed as being dominated by a relic from a bygone era of patriarchal feudal societies.

Typically, the founding fathers of such plantations faced formidable challenges: the region's periodic droughts and barren soil demanded a tenacious resilience in the face of adversity. The values embodied by these settlers – resilience and an accompanying sense of individualism – are prized by Northeasterners and are revered to the present day in the region's folklore. The demise of the Northeast's plantation society in the early twentieth century stems from a conflict between these traditional regional values and the forces of modernization. *Fogo morto* depicts this clash thematically through two central conflicts, one political and the other sociological, and, like *Vidas sêcas*, it portrays the conflict stylistically, through experiments with traditional modes of narration.

Fogo morto reveals the sociological consequences of the conflict between tradition and modernization by focusing on the plight of José Amaro, a Santa Fe tenant evicted by Lula de Holanda. Lula resides in the 'big house' at the centre of the plantation and typifies a phenomenon described by Freyre in *Sobrados e Mucambos*: an outsider marries into land ownership and aspires to the accompanying luxuries, but lacks the resilience and dedication necessary to sustain a plantation. Lula surrounds himself with luxuries absurdly incongruous with the local environment – most notably, a grand piano for his daughters and an ostentatious carriage for himself – and sits idly by while his Santa Fe plantation falls into ruin. As the victim of Lula's decadence, Amaro typifies traditional Northeast values: he dreams of taking revenge on Lula by aiding Silvino, leader of a local band of outlaws or *cangaceiros*. (The *cangaceiro* is the traditional Northeastern folk hero that Távora's Cabeleira was modeled after; he embodies the Northeastern values of individualism, resilience, and disrespect for social convention.) Amaro's dream of revenge seems to be realized when Silvino and his gang plunder the mansion; however, the bandits only flee, leaving the feudal system that enslaves Amaro intact.

While the plot of *Fogo morto* echoes Freyre's political and sociological themes, stylistically the novel does not mimic the sociologist's authoritative perspective. Instead, Lins do Rêgo employs innovative modernist poetics to portray from within the claustrophobic effect of the encroaching external forces that threaten both the cultural identity of the region and the individual identities of its inhabitants. The novel is divided into three seemingly independent sections: sections one and three describe events covering approximately one month in 1911, and section two looks back a generation to describe the founding of the plantation by Captain Tomás. By focalizing the narration of the first section entirely through José Amaro, a character whose paranoid delusions border on the psychotic, Lins do Rêgo creates a surreal fictional world distinctly at odds with the well-ordered universe of his earlier realistic fiction. Although the focalization varies in the novel's remaining two sections, from alternating internal focalizations to more traditional nonfocalized narration, this opening section establishes a conflict between the internal 'world' of the character and a threatening external world; this conflict continues through the rest of the novel, and it mirrors the political and cultural tensions between the Northeast and the forces emanating from a threatening external world.

Fogo morto's first section (approximately one-third of the novel) presents a claustrophobic world defined by the severely limited perception of José Amaro. The novel opens with Amaro in his leather shop; before him is a window overlooking the street, through which he is conversing with a passing neighbour, and behind him, in the dark recesses of the house's interior, are Amaro's wife and daughter. They remain for the most part an indistinct murmur in the background; the neighbouring land exists only as perceived by Amaro through his window, or as seen by him in the obscure light of his nocturnal wanderings; and the world beyond the Santa Fe plantation is only vaguely sketched in through second-hand accounts related to him by passing travellers.

The few passages in the first section that describe the natural environment beyond the walls of Amaro's house only serve to emphasize the conflict between his internal world and the threatening world outside. We repeatedly get glimpses of sunlight, flowers, and songbirds through Amaro's window or doorway, but these glimpses are immediately contrasted with the dark torment of Amaro's interior world. A typical description begins with what appears to be the voice of a traditional omniscient narrator, who tells us that 'outside it was a beautiful May afternoon' (16). After a brief description of some local flora, Amaro's wife passes in front of his window, and it becomes clear that the description is focalized from within the leather shop. The narration then turns inward to describe Amaro's thoughts: we are told that 'he could not hide his hatred for her' (16) and that he vents his frustration by pounding furiously on the leather before him. Similarly, references to a songbird outside Amaro's shack only serve to heighten the portrayal of his inner torment: following an idyllic description of a bird singing in the sunshine the narration switches abruptly to the contrasting fury of Amaro's own heartbeat, which 'pounded with the violence of a burst dam' (47).

Alienated from the world around him, Amaro retreats to a mythical world defined by local folklore. In Amaro's imagination, Silvino, the leader of the *cangaceiros*, takes on the stature of a local folk hero (a role filled by Cabeleira in Távora's novel, and by Antonio Conselheiro in Cunha's *Os sertões*) and becomes the 'saviour' who would deliver Amaro from this 'world of perdition' (49). Amaro's dreams, however, are not realized; when he finally gets up the courage to leave his hut under cover of darkness and attempts to join Silvino's men he is overcome by an epileptic fit and has to be carried back to his shack. The *cangaceiros* finally do come to Amaro's aid by overrunning Lula's plantation house, but by then not only is it too late to save the plantation, but the nomadic *cangaceiros* cannot offer any viable alternative to Lula's despotic rule: they plunder the mansion and leave it in a shambles before deserting the region.

Section one establishes a conflict between the personal, interior world of a character and the exterior world of his environment, as well as a conflict between traditional regional values and a contradictory modern world. Amaro is alienated from those around him: his wife fears him, his daughter is insane, and his neighbours believe he is a werewolf. Condemned to a solitary existence as the plantation saddle-maker, Amaro loses even that last remnant of identity when Lula evicts him from the plantation. As the only world he knows collapses around him, Amaro seeks refuge in a surreal world defined by local folklore, but there finds no relief from the encroaching forces that eventually engulf his world.

At the opening of section two the narrative focus 'zooms out' to tell the history of Santa Fe from a distance, with the significant dates and names provided in the impersonal voice of an external observer. The narration occasionally returns to internal focalization to portray isolation similar to Amaro's in the opening section: husbands are ostracized from family and community (Lula, Vitorino, and Tomás), and wives are alienated from cruel husbands and insane daughters (Amélia, Adriana, and Mariquina). These internally focalized narrations are fragmentary, but the effect is the same as in section one: brief passages focalized through each of these characters show interior personal 'worlds' in conflict with the exterior world, conflicts which mirror a broader conflict between region and world.

One character is an anomaly in this world of introspective isolation: Captain Vitorino does not barricade himself in the private world of his own thoughts, but takes his battle for political reform to the streets of Pilar. His exploits are not narrated from the confines of a paranoid and deluded consciousness, but from the more traditional perspective of a third-person observer. Critics have praised this character as a redeeming thread of continuity in an otherwise fragmentary narrative; Vitorino's pursuit of honour and dignity in the face of a contrary world is frequently compared to that of Cervantes' Don Quixote, and the character is often cited as Lins do Rêgo's most valuable contribution to Brazilian literature.[8] If regionalism is the novel's unifying purpose, however, Vitorino is not an anomaly at all: his character is merely one variation on the conflict between region and world that informs the entire novel. Rather than isolate himself inside his house, Vitorino takes his battle against the encroaching borders of the outside world to the streets. Beaten by police and bandits alike and ridiculed by the politicians, Vitorino takes on the traditional foes of Northeastern autonomy, but with no more success than Amaro and the novel's more reclusive characters. Vitorino's courageous fight against overwhelming odds typifies the individualism glorified in Northeast folklore, but his ultimate defeat suggests that the pride and determination of the community's founders belong to a bygone era, that they are no match for the political and economic forces of the modern world.

Fogo morto incorporates all the regional themes institutionalized by previous generations of Northeast literature, including bandits, mysticism, drought, and the heroic resilience of the *cangaceiros*. But by portraying the world of his novel from the point of view of the region's native inhabitants, Lins do Rêgo offers an alternative to the idealistic glorification of the region established by observers from the outside, from Alencar's romantic primitivism and Tavora's realism to Euclides da Cunha's journalistic chronicle of the Canudos uprising. *Fogo morto* questions traditional perceptions of regional culture by drawing a parallel between the universal confrontation between self and world and the confrontation between region and world. The death of Amaro and the concurrent death of the fires that fuel the plantations sugar-cane refinery (the 'fogo morto' of the novel's title) signify the final defeat of individualism and the victory of the federalist forces to the South over the regional values of the Northeast.

While introducing formal innovations that break with realist tradition, *Fogo morto* succeeds in reflecting a crisis of national identity that transcends the regional concerns of the Northeast. The Week of Modern Art in 1922 shook the cultural community with its futurism, cubism, and other borrowings from the European avant garde. Following the revolution of 1930, and the successive rewritings of the constitution that gave increasingly centralized power to a military dictator, the country's political identity was unstable, and rapid industrialization together with the disappearance of the agrarian economy on which the country was founded resulted in further social upheaval. Having long since lost its secure identity as a colonial possession, Brazil was finally forced to face its selfhood, and José Amaro's struggle to maintain his identity while his world closes in around him reflects the broader struggle of a nation to establish and preserve an autonomous identity in the face of a changing world.

Brazil's Northeast authors of the 1930s and 1940s are typical of the *regionalismo* movements that sprang up throughout South America during that period. Although such a cohesive and sustained coalition of regionalist authors would be almost unknown in North America (The Fugitive/Agrarians would be the only example), individual authors in Canada and the United States would also depict regional cultures threatened by political conflicts that mirrored the larger struggles of New World nations to come to terms with their selfhood. These authors all responded to the conflicting forces of similarity and difference, and local conditions would give each of the conflicts a distinct character.

LA TIERRA PRÓDIGA

Mexico has a distinctive national character derived partly from its isolation: it is separated from its neighbours to the south by a narrow land bridge and from its neighbours to the north by linguistic and cultural differences. Mexico also has a distinctive cultural history, arising from a particularly bloody and violent history that predates the conquest. Early twentieth-century Mexican authors integrated the country's isolation and bloody past with more recent themes of revolution and corruption. Since the Revolution of 1910, Mexican culture has been consumed by the need to explain, justify, or otherwise make sense of the country's violent past and its seemingly endless cycle of tyranny and rebellion.

One of the most centralized societies in the world (about 20 per cent of the country's eighty million inhabitants live in Mexico City),[9] Mexico does not have a notable history of literary regionalism. Nevertheless, among prominent twentieth-century authors a surprising number are natives of the Pacific coast region contained within the borders of the state of Jalisco. One of the most prominent of the Jalisco authors is Agustín Yáñez, and in many of his works historical consciousness and national identity are tied to a very distinct sense of place. In his novel *La tierra pródiga*, Yáñez brings his concern with the country's violent past to a story set in the modern-day state of Jalisco.

The novel's protagonist, Ricardo Guerra, stumbles upon an uncultivated tract of land bordering on the ocean and enlists the aid of government officials and local inhabitants in a grandiose scheme to develop a tourist resort of unparalleled luxury. Through deception and manipulation, Guerra takes control of the region and appoints himself its sole representative. Then he insinuates his way into elite social circles in the capital city of Guadalajara, where he procures promises of massive economic aid. His plan backfires, though, when, overcome by greed, he begins eliminating his neighbours from the development scheme, and as the region falls into chaos, the federal sponsors back out of his plan. At the novel's conclusion, Guerra rages impotently while bulldozers and heavy equipment stand idle, apparently poised to begin development at the direction of the central planners who have pushed the local boss aside.

Guerra typifies the *cacique* of rural communities throughout Latin America: almost every region has its local boss who through deceit and cunning becomes the self-appointed lord and benefactor of the community. Through references to the Spanish conquest of Mexico, however, Yáñez presents the rapacious appetites of this *cacique* as something he has inherited from Mexican history. Even more specifically, Yáñez gives modern-day Mexico's preoccupation with the conquest and the revolution a regional twist by linking Guerra's greed to specific topographic and climatic features of the region.

Several passages in *La tierra pródiga* are full of local-colour details, but their effect is quite different from the effect of realist catalogues of local artefacts. The lists of local details in *La tierra pródiga* are overwhelming; they exaggerate the technique of cataloguing to the point of self-consciously demonstrating the futility of any attempt to capture all the details of regional identity. In a single breathless stream of nouns, for example, we are provided with an overwhelming list of local fauna, ranging from flies and mosquitoes to parrots and toucans, coyotes and leopards (I refrain from translating; many of these names are drawn from a regional lexicon and have no direct English equivalent):

Acechanzas de moscas, mosquitos, bobos, jejenes, avispas, hormigas, güinas, garrapatas, tarántulas, alacranes, víboras, más el reino de caza mayor: tigrillos, onzas, lobos, leopardos, bajo la gracia de clarines, clandrias, cardenales, carpinteros, codornices, guacos, güilotas, gorriones, citos, queleles, jilgueros, alondras, zenzontles, tordos, torcazas, tucanes, tildíos, mirlos, ruiseñores, palomas, verdines, zanates, zorzales, a los gritos de loros, chicharras y cotorras, a los nocturnos grillos, ranas, lechuzas y salamandras, en el hálito cenital o en la noche sofocada: reto al sol de águilas, aguilillas y gavilanes; curvas torvas de zopilotes y cuervos. (62)

But local colour in *La tierra pródiga* is not limited to lists of regional artefacts: some descriptive passages convey a more personal attachment to the region. A description of the area's beaches, for example, is one of the most moving testimonies to a sense of place to be found anywhere in New World regionalism. As Guerra stands on a promontory gazing at the scene below, readers are treated to a view of

expansive beaches, seen from above as vast fans, slowly undulating, mother-of-pearl fans, spread-out, tipped with a foam filigree, slowly undulating, brief, graceful, thin beaches, encased in rugged granite: beaches whispering with the sound of pebbles and shells; open seas, enraged, roaring; fury of the waves futilely contained by hostile rocks; swollen, raging waves collapsing in a tremendous roar of pearls; epiphany of colours: deep blue, green, turquoise, sky-blue, peaking in crests, extending in folds, in fine lace, in bubbling flecks of white ... (56)

Such lyrical descriptions extend for several pages in parts of *La tierra pródiga*, but the novel does more than just sing the praises of the author's native region: it also tells the story of one man's attempt to dominate and possess a region, and of his battle to retain that possession in the face of forces beyond his control. Regionalism takes on a sinister, horrifying aspect in *La tierra pródiga* when the character develops more than a fond affection for a particular place. The region's spectacular beauty excites violent and insatiable passions in Guerra, passions that lead to violent conflict.

The plot begins with Guerra's first contact with the region, when in his late adolescence he is given a message to deliver to the coastal town of Chamela. Prior to that momentous errand, Guerra is an *alteño*, a high-lander living on the inland plain abutting the coastal region. We are told that through his early years the coastal region had been a constant but peripheral presence in Guerra's life: though he had never seen the ocean, 'it lured him ... He breathed it in the warm humidity, in the salt breeze from afar, in the ubiquitous circumambient sensuality' (89). For those who live in direct contact with the region – referred to as *la tierra caliente* – the climate permeates the very rhythm of life: the air is 'filled with interminable rhythms, natural pulsation of the earth, of the warm climate' (245).

With machete in hand, Guerra plunges into the region, in quest of 'the inaccessible heart of *la tierra caliente*' (135). His first contact with the region is compared to the taming of a beast – a comparison with unmis-takable sexual overtones: as Guerra hacks a path through the jungle he feels 'the same emotion as when he first mounted a wild mare, hands buried in the bristling mane, overcome with fury, frantic in the struggle, in the relentless punishment of the rebellious female' (89). This sexual imagery is the prevalent metaphor in the novel. Although the region is described at times as an untamed beast or an uncultivated garden, it is above all the region's sexual allure that motivates the protagonist to possess it.

This conflict between man and region is attributed to the cultural differences separating the *alteñas* and the *abajeñas*, or lowlanders. Seen through the strict Christian morality of Guerra's upbringing, the *abajeñas* are wild, promiscuous, animal-like. Guerra is shocked by their frankness and their easy-going manner; in one scene, he is irritated beyond endurance at the sight of them dancing. Nevertheless, Guerra marries a lowland woman, and her appeal is unmistakable: we are told that he associates her with the wild beauty of the region, and that upon meeting Elena in one of his early forays into the region he is surprised by 'the discovery that he was in love. Doubly. Nature and woman were one' (96–7). From that moment on, Guerra is guided by a belief that he repeats, mantra-like, throughout the novel: 'If I dominate one I will dominate the other.'

Guerra's furious assault on the region is fuelled by an insatiable passion, for he is impelled not by any obtainable goal, but by desire itself. His first act of possession is to name the land, and he names each point after one of his seemingly innumerable sexual conquests. As he recalls his recitation of names to a recent visitor – 'Punta Elena, punta Margarita, punta Rosana, punta Catalina, punta Ida, punta Marta, punta Elise' – Guerra remembers remarking to the visitor, 'Each one has the name of a woman.' Guerra then reflects on the illusive nature of the object of his desire: he recalls that he had wanted to say that each point bears the name not of a woman, but 'of an illusion'; he realises that all of those names represent 'desires that germinate but never flower ... fleeting shadows of dreamed-of pleasures' (71).

In *La tierra pródiga* Yáñez does more than describe local flora and fauna. Just as Távora had done in his portrayal of the Brazilian Northeast, Yáñez draws on regional history in his depiction of the Mexican west coast. Unlike Távora, though, Yáñez does not strive for a literal recreation of historic events; instead he suggests an allegorical parallel between the events narrated in his novel and earlier attempts to cultivate the region. This figurative reference has farther-reaching implications: by interspersing the narrative of Guerra's conquest of the region with historical refrences to the Spanish conquest, Yáñez suggests a parallel between the tale of Guerra's domination of the region and historical accounts of the Spanish conquest.

In one passage, Medellín, the engineer whom Guerra has enlisted in his development scheme, recalls the history of the region as it has come to him through picture books and popular literature. First, Medellín recalls a painting of Nuño Beltrán de Guzmán, leader of the original Spanish expedition into the region. Painted by an indigenous artist, the scene of Guzmán's death is overseen by the flaming serpent of Aztec mythology, 'an augury of death, misery, desolation and ruin' (166). Medellín then recalls an account written by a Jesuit priest, who had described a colonial landowner as suffering an earthly hell, enduring the indignities of a harsh and uncultivated land and the threat of heathen dogs awaiting their chance to tear him to pieces. Finally, he considers the historical parallel with Guerra's arrival in the region: 'After the Spanish conquerors had passed through, leaving the echoes of their force resounding through the region, and had left the region lost and forgotten for centuries, [Guerra] had come along and discovered it, single-handedly conquering it inch by inch, impelled by the patriotic toil of creating new centres of production, in the service of national progress' (163–4). From the engineer's point of view, nothing has changed in nearly five centuries; the conquerors' dreams of gold and converted souls have simply been replaced with modern-day dreams of 'centres of production' and 'national progress.'

While on an allegorical level references to the region's Spanish colonizers impart a broader significance to the rise and fall of Ricardo Guerra, on a more literal level Guerra's tyranny is attributed to a very specific source in local geography. A voice belonging to the region itself, to 'the echoes of the shadows and the consciences of the hidden recesses,' describes a history of men driven mad by the region. The voice refers to 'the fickle disposition of those bewitched by *la tierra caliente*, those who walk across its swamps, who sleep beneath its venomous plants, those stung by tarantulas, serpents, and vampires, and those who see gold in the sand and in the rivers, those who tear the guts out of Christians in search of pearls, and the madmen who level hills and forests, driven by a thirst that devours them, bewitched by *la tierra caliente*' (313).

In *La tierra pródiga*, Yáñez gives us regionalism from a different perspective. Details of local colour and lyrical passages attesting to the region's beauty are evidence of the author's undeniable sense of place and of his personal affinity with the region. But through Ricardo Guerra,

Yáñez portrays a perverted regionalism in which regionalist forces lead to a violent clash between man and region. This perverted regionalism offers an insight into the particularly rapacious and bloody conquest of the region and, by extension, that of Mexico itself.

The novel's conclusion is ambiguous. Guerra is left, like Lula de Holanda in *Fogo morto*, raving impotently as forces of modernization close in on the region. As bulldozers sit idling on the periphery of the region, it would seem that industry and capital are poised to bring the region – and by analogy the country – up to date with the rest of the Western world. But at the novel's conclusion neither Guerra nor the the central planners have succeeded in imposing their will on the region. Yáñez's ironic reference to 'national progress' and his cryptic references to indigenous forces suggest another possibility: that the central planners housed in the state capital of Guadalajara are no more likely to conquer the region than were earlier forces dispatched from Spain by way of Mexico City.

La tierra pródiga's story of a failed real-estate speculator has enormous ramifications. Guerra fails to impose his will on the region and allegorical references suggest that the central planners from Guadalajara may fare no better. The implication is that 'conquest' may in fact be a misnomer, that indigenous forces – the bewitching forces of *la tierra caliente* – continue to prevail over a perpetual cycle of domination and ruin. As we shall see in chapter 5, the intriguing possibility that is hinted at in *La tierra pródiga* would be developed more explicitly by Carlos Fuentes in *La región más transparente*.

CHAPTER FOUR

The Poetics of Place

SPATIAL FORM

Discussing regionalism and modernism in the North American context is problematic because the prevailing schools of modernist criticism tend either to equate heightened aesthetic awareness with a corresponding decrease in referential capacity, or to dismiss innovations in prose poetics altogether as mere trickery at best, or, at worst, as deliberate obfuscations that can be untangled only through rigorous 'close reading.' The perceived divorce of modernist poetics from real-world reference is largely due to a spurious distinction between poetics and thematics that has been perpetuated by a debate between Joseph Frank and critics of his theory of 'spatial form in literature.'[1]

Frank coined the term 'spatial form' to describe certain early twentieth-century works of fiction that reject traditional narrative syntax. He reasoned that because these works disrupt the diachronic sequentiality inherent in both linguistic syntax and narrative plot, they might be called 'atemporal.' From the assumption that 'non-diachronic' means 'atemporal,' Frank proceeded to the conclusion that these works can therefore be considered 'spatial.' One of Frank's most outspoken critics is Frank Kermode, who argues that we can arrive at a work's meaning only through a chronological process of reading from beginning to end (he refers to meaning as a work's 'wisdom plot'), and that modernist works are, therefore, no less temporal than any other kind of literature.[2] This debate pits poetics against thematics, with Frank, on the one side, arguing that as a result of modernism's disruption of traditional syntax, what he describes as 'synchronic relations *within* the text' take precedence over external referentiality ('An Answer to Critics' 235), and Kermode and others, on the other side, arguing that all works arrive at meaning dia-chronically and modernist works are, therefore, no more 'spatial' than any other literature.

Frank's theory of 'spatial form' responds to a verifiable phenomenon: neither Kermode nor any of Frank's other detractors would deny that certain early twentieth-century works disrupt the linear syntax of tradi-tional prose narrative. The technique stems from an effort to mimic synchronic cognitive processes, and its development in prose fiction can be traced back to attempts to mimic the effect of nineteenth-century Impressionist painting. Underlying the stylistic strategies of such modern-ist authors as Proust, Joyce, and Faulkner is the desire to counteract what Henri Bergson described as 'the deeply rooted habit of extending time in space' (93). These modernist authors strive to portray in their fiction an alternative to the traditional view of linear temporality, an alternative described by the Bergsonian term 'pure durée,' a synchronic 'mutual penetration of facts of consciousness' (82). Frank's theory recognizes the Bergsonian 'durée,' which might, as Frank suggests, be described as synchronic rather than diachronic. From that point, however, Frank's theory takes an unfortunate turn by equating 'synchronic' with 'atem-poral,' and 'atemporality' with the negation of real-world reference. In fact, synchrony is by no means a denial of temporality, and its use as a syntactic structuring principle in narrative fiction by no means entails the denial, or even the diminution, of real-world historicity. We have already seen in Ramos and Lins do Rêgo rudimentary experiments in linking regional identity to non-diachronic temporality, and in this chapter we will see more fully realized depictions of fictional worlds that are defined by non-diachronic temporality.

Both sides in the clamorous debate over whether the fiction of Faulkner, Joyce, and others is any more 'spatial' than more traditional realist narratives perpetuate a false dichotomy based on the assumption that a work of art must reflect *either* the internal workings of human cognition *or* the external data of real-world historicity. Regionalism was a casualty of this false dichotomy, for the common assumption that experiments with non-linear syntax must be non-referential denied the possibility of modernist regionalism. Only those works that employed anachronistic realist techniques continued to be recognized as regionalist, and from the early decades of the twentieth century to the present day, regionalism has been relegated to the periphery of North American literature and criticism.

In recent years William Spanos has outlined an approach that offers a means of breaking the impasse between 'spatialists' and 'temporalists' by presenting an alternative to the diachronic model of historicity that both Frank and his detractors are bound by. Spanos describes the non-diachronic temporality portrayed by certain modernist works as a representation of the individual's confrontation with a perpetually displaced present, reflecting a 'middle or existential state, the state of Becoming ... between beginning and end in time' ('Modern Literary Criticism' 101). The disruption of linear syntax in such works need not entail a denial of temporality; it need only offer an alternative to linear temporality. Coining a spatial metaphor of his own, Spanos suggests that all narrative works exhibit a 'time-shape' of one kind or another – be it linear, cyclical, or spiral, to name just a few possibilities – and that far from denying real-world representation, this 'time-shape' necessarily reflects an author's immediate confrontation with real-world historicity.

In regionalist fiction, this 'time-shape' will reflect a very particular view of being-in-the-world, derived from a distinct local reality. We have seen how realist authors strove to reinforce ontological borders from the external vantage point of a disinterested observer. The shortcomings of this approach were hinted at by the characters in Norris's *The Octopus*, who found that the world around them refused to be contained in such rigid frames. The modernist regionalist reverses the realist approach, confronting the borders that define regional identity from within and drawing a parallel between the always-threatened borders of regional identity and what Spanos describes as 'the uncertain boundaries of human existence' ('Modern Literary Criticism' 88).

Kermode and Frank (and the adherents of both sides in the 'temporalist'/'spatialist' debate) are mired in what W.J.T. Mitchell refers to as a 'seemingly hopeless tangle of spatial metaphors which riddle the languages of criticism' (281). Spanos effectively untangles the confusion by offering an alternative to the diachronic model that such critics as Frank and Kermode had been trying to impose on non-diachronic literature. Mitchell breaks through the critical impasse by providing an analytic paradigm capable of accounting for a plurality of 'time-shapes'; he describes four levels of spatiality in fiction that encompass both real-world representation and patterns of syntactic structure. The first level of spatiality Mitchell identifies is the physical existence of the document itself, which, he explains, was more significant in the era of illuminated manuscripts than it is today. Mitchell's second level corresponds to thematic representation, or what he calls the 'descriptive' level, 'in which we attend to the world which is represented, imitated, or signified in a work' (283). The third level corresponds to what is commonly referred to as narrative 'structure' or 'form'; on this level 'patterns of coherence' are determined by a 'principle which governs the order or sequence of presentation in a text' (284). The fourth level corresponds to the 'metaphysics which lies behind a story told about *this* world in *this* particular way,' or what Mitchell refers to, admittedly for lack of a better term, as 'meaning' (285). According to Mitchell's model, there is no real disagreement between Kermode and Frank: they are talking about two separate levels of spatiality. Frank's 'spatial form' refers to a structural technique that disrupts the linear causality inherent in realist form, while Kermode's 'wisdom plot' leads to a 'synchronic' moment of cognition in which meaning is derived. Mitchell's second level divorces referentiality from prescriptive models of temporality, leaving open the possibility of represented worlds portraying either diachronic or synchronic historicity.

The romantic and realist regionalist novels examined in chapters 1 and 2 relied on what Bergson described as the 'homogeneous durée' of diachronic time. In the early and mid-nineteenth century, regionalists such as Cooper and Alencar strove to place regional identity within the context of civilization's 'forward' progress, and later regionalists such as Távora, Cunha, and Norris depicted regions as a 'chapter in the history of the Earth' (Cunha 295), or a 'passing phase of history' (Norris, *Octopus* 10). All of these nineteenth-century regionalist authors shaped their represented worlds according to a diachronic plot. We saw in chapter 3 how *Vidas sècas* and *Fogo morto* present tentative exercises in linking the disruption of linear chronology to distinct regional forces.

Not only had considerable innovations been introduced in the poetics of narrative fiction since Norris's *The Octopus*, but by the 1920s and 1930s North American attitudes towards regionalism had undergone equally dramatic changes. In the early decades of the twentieth century, regionalism no longer was seen as the salvation of American literature, as Garland had described it, but as just the opposite: a sign of provincialism that barred American writing from the pantheon of world literature. A brief look at the politics and poetics of a group of renegade Southern critics and writers who branded themselves the 'Fugitives' will provide the context for Faulkner's regionalist use of modernist 'spatial form.'

FUGITIVE/AGRARIAN POLITICS

In the 1920s and 1930s regionalism suddenly became problematic for U.S. writers. The local fiction that Howells had envisioned as the future of

American art was now seen not only as aesthetically anachronistic, but also as politically subversive. The contradictory forces of regional difference and national unity – which Howells had blithely dismissed with his assumption that the former was obviously subservient to the latter – broke out into the open, and heated debates ensued pitting regionalists against those advocating national unity. The debates galvanized what had previously been a loose grouping of local-colour artists, who now for the first time were given the name 'regionalist.' Referring to the terms 'region' and 'regionalism,' Donald Davidson noted in 1938 that 'the advent of the new terms is in itself the fact of prime importance, suggesting as it does that American criticism has recently encountered a problem it was not prepared to face or even to name' (275). Regionalism had indeed become a problem; authors and critics alike seemed to be looking for the 'great American novel,' and despite conflicting ideas about what form that novel would take, the prevailing consensus seemed to be that whatever it was, it would not be regionalist.

The most ambitious quest for the American novel was John Dos Passos's *U.S.A.* trilogy, a sprawling collage of 'newsreel' fragments and 'camera-eye' images that sweep the country, defying specificity of place. For Theodore Dreiser the quest meant that a murder in rural Missouri was not just a local incident: it symbolized a greater, national tragedy (which he would later chronicle in his novel *An American Tragedy*). Other novelists seemed to feel that the American novel could be written anywhere *except* the one place that was essential to regionalism: home. Fitzgerald would follow Hemingway to France, and others, like Thomas Wolfe, would leave home to congregate around their publishers in New York. The prevailing trend was clearly away from regionalism, and although regionalism's opponents were not united under any single name, John Crowe Ransom offered a number of terms to describe these prevailing anti-regionalist forces: 'cosmopolitanism, progressivism, industrialism, free trade, interregionalism, internationalism, eclecticism, liberal education, the federation of the world, or simple rootlessness' (293–4).

In the United States, regionalism survived in the 1920s and 1930s through small literary magazines. While national magazines swelled their circulation figures by publishing stories by cosmopolitan writers like Fitzgerald and Hemingway, regional magazines, often with readerships only in the hundreds, provided local fiction for local audiences. These small magazines did not present a unified opposition to the anti-regionalist majority, but for the most part editors quietly catered to a local market without explicitly voicing a counter-argument to the reigning

anti-regionalist sentiment. One of these small magazines, however, attracted a core of political activists who went on to form the only overtly
political regionalist movement twentieth-century U.S. literature has ever
known. In the early 1920s, a group of young writers that included John
Crowe Ransom, Allen Tate, Donald Davidson, and Robert Penn Warren
gathered at Vanderbilt University in Nashville; together they published a
magazine called the *Fugitive*.

The magazine itself was short-lived, but its contributors went on to
defend regionalism in publications with such inflammatory titles as *I'll
Take My Stand*, *The Attack on Leviathan*, and *Who Owns America? A New
Declaration of Independence*. The *Fugitive* writers – or the Agrarians, as they
later came to be known – were united primarily by political motives, but
their defence of regionalism went beyond merely resurrecting the
North/South rivalry that had in the previous century led to the Civil War.
Although an undeniable distaste for the North and Northern ways underlies the rhetoric of the Agrarians, their enemy was not the North in
particular, but a general phenomenon that Davidson refers to as 'regional
imperialism.' Davidson declared that 'regionalists would seek to eliminate
the possibility of regional imperialism in any quarter ... If they can help
it, they would not permit ... the tyranny of the majority' (27). The Agrarians were not only defending Southern regionalism, but were proposing
regionalism in general as an alternative to the 'tyranny' of such cultural
and economic centres as New York.

Davidson traces the popular perception of a national literature back to
the previous century, when the same 'old men' Garland had described
as clinging to 'crumbling idols' had used nationalism as, in Davidson's
words, 'an attempt to rationalize a cultural tradition which it became
almost a point of honor to label as a distinctive possession' (272). The
British had used this reasoning, Davidson continues, to justify the evolution of an increasingly pompous national literature: 'If the modern
Englishman had evolved from a one-cell organism up to the state of
Victorian complexity represented in Mr. Gladstone, then English literature had to be exhibited as mounting nobly up the evolutionary ladder
from amoebic verse to the lofty periods of Alfred, Lord Tennyson' (272).
According to Davidson, this same logic led Americans to view regionalism
as a minor step towards a great literature: just as a great nation had
evolved from a smattering of colonies, so a great national literature would
evolve from lesser regional literatures. Not only was such thinking outdated, Davidson argued, but it was entirely unsuited to the American political and cultural context: 'Regionalism is a name for a condition under

which the national American literature exists as a literature: that is, its constant tendency to decentralize rather than to centralize; or to correct overcentralization by conscious decentralization' (269).

John Crowe Ransom's 'The Aesthetics of Regionalism' outlines a defence of regionalism very similar to Alencar's regionalist manifesto, with the significant exception that the North American introduces a break from the cultural homogeneity sought by Alencar. Ransom's theory begins with economic necessity; when a community is first settled, its means of production are determined by locally available materials. As in the first stage of Alencar's three-part evolutionary scheme, 'human nature at this stage is chiefly biological, and raw' (Ransom 296) and is therefore susceptible to the influence of environment. Ransom's theory, however, combines the second and third stages of Alencar's evolutionary model – in which primitive society first absorbs the stamp of local environment and then acquires culture through contact with an external society – into a single stage. According to Ransom's theory, culture arises spontaneously and is entirely local: 'As a community slowly adapts its life to the geography of the region, a thing happens which is almost miraculous ... As the economic patterns become perfected and easy, they cease to be merely economic and become gradually aesthetic' (296). The elimination of Alencar's third phase – the intervention of an external culture – is an important innovation: for the first time, New World regionalism is credited with spawning an indigenous, local culture, rather than aspiring to a pre-formed culture defined by great civilizations of the past.

For Ransom, regional art is the *only* art; he sees eclecticism as the opposite of regionalism, and while for him regionalism is synonymous with culture, eclecticism is synonymous with everything that opposes culture: 'In contrast with the regional view ... eclectic minds are doubtless good for something, but they are very dangerous for the health of the arts' (299). Ransom generally associates eclecticism with urbanization, but he suggests that not all cities are necessarily built 'upon indifferent and eclectic foundations' (299–300). Without specifically referring to urban regionalism, Ransom implies that a city that develops naturally around local commerce and that does not deny its local history can maintain its regional aesthetic.

Ransom is inflexible about one traditional characteristic of regionalism: that regional identity is accessible only to a native of the region. According to his definition, outsiders can recognize a region only after Ransom's two-part cycle is completed. When a regional community has made the transition from economic subsistence to aesthetic distinctiveness, 'the region is now "made" in the vulgar sense ... that the curious and eclectic populations of far-away capitals will mark it on their maps.' Ransom believes that regional identity is instilled in local inhabitants long before that moment: 'But for the regionalists who live in the region it is made already, because they have taken it into themselves by assimilation' (297–8). This personal sense of regional identity is derived not only from 'the physical region, the nature who has always given them sustenance,' but also from 'the historic community which has dwelt in this region all these generations,' and which has developed distinctive patterns of communal life (298).

Robert Penn Warren suggests innovative ways of portraying this distinct cultural identity when he hints at an alternative to realist poetics in his praise of some contemporary regionalists whose works 'represent deviations from the ordinary fictional norm of reported actuality' (*Southern Harvest* xvi). These writers, according to Warren, 'have attempted to assume the responsibility of creating characters from the inside out; they have not been content with the routine process of penetrating the surface of reported actuality.' In another essay, Warren criticizes traditional regionalist fiction for treating specificity of time and place as mutually exclusive. He describes local-colour fiction as merely a superficial treatment of local space divorced from historical context. To Warren this kind of descriptive fiction 'does not provide a framework in which human action has more than immediate and adventitious significance' ('Not Local Color' 154). Warren identifies another kind of regionalism in historical romances that capture the manners of an era, but he says that these ignore the vital interaction between human communities and regional environments; in such works, Warren explains, 'manners tend to be substituted for value, and costume and *décor* for an essential relationship between man and his background' ('Not Local Color' 154). What these traditional kinds of regionalism – descriptive and historical – ignore, Warren claims, is that both setting and historical context are essential to regionalism, but that neither alone is sufficient. To Warren, both local-colour realism and nostalgic novels of manners deny the important fact that for the regionalist 'time and place are one thing' ('Not Local Color' 154). This necessary interdependence, or 'interpenetration,' to use Bergson's term, of time and place is echoed in Davidson's insistence that regionalism must be more than a catalogue of local details, that rather than 'dwell among the artifacts' belonging to a region, the regionalist author must 'from his region, confront the total and moving world' (277). The key word in Davidson's reference is *moving*; regionalism, according to him, must not only acknowledge a region's existence within the world, but recognize that the world within which the region exists is not a static, immutable object.

The Fugitive/Agrarians made an important contribution to our understanding of regionalism. The *Fugitive* was born of a distaste for the kind of sentimental nostalgia that had dominated Southern writing since the Civil War. The Agrarians insisted that regionalism meant more than adhering to local topics; that its tone did not have to be romantic and retrospective; that it was not antithetical to nationalism; and, as Warren and Davidson suggested, that it meant something more than superficial description of external reality. These contributions have been largely ignored in North American criticism for several reasons, not the least of which is that the short-lived Fugitive and Agrarian movements were quickly overshadowed by debates over the New Criticism, in which Ransom, Warren, and other former Fugitives figured prominently. Their contributions to a definition of regionalism are also largely discredited by the fact that the Agrarians themselves offered little in the way of alternatives to the sentimental local-colour fiction they derided. Poems like Ransom's 'Bells for John Whiteside's Daughter' or Tate's 'Ode to the Confederate Dead' may be less superficial and sentimental than those of the poets' contemporaries, but to today's readers the difference is a matter more of degree than of substance.

The only novelist to emerge from the Fugitive/Agrarians was Robert Penn Warren, and only his first novel, *Night Rider*, might be considered regionalist in that, like *Os sertões*, it draws its material from a historical conflict in which peasants took up arms against forces dispatched to the region from a distant urban centre. The combatants in *Night Rider* are not religious fanatics and federal soldiers, as in *Os sertões*, but sharecroppers and agents from a cartel of tobacco companies based in the North. The novel succeeds in portraying thematically a confrontation between regional autonomy and 'the tyranny of the majority,' but it fails to counter this same homogenizing force on the level of language and narrative structure. *Night Rider* offers no alternative to the static progression of discrete time segments that prevented the fiction of Cunha, Távora, and Norris from portraying regional identity as difference on the level of represented reality.

The regionalism described by the Fugitive/Agrarians would find a more successful practitioner in a writer who at the time was contributing short stories to another small southern magazine entitled the *Double Dealer*.

FAULKNER'S POETICS OF PLACE

Although Warren refers to several authors in his praise of innovative regionalists, it seems relatively clear in retrospect that he had one author in particular in mind. His reference to writers who 'have not been content with the routine process of penetrating the surface of reported actuality' does not seem quite as well suited to Katherine Anne Porter, Erskine Caldwell, Caroline Gordon, or others he mentions, as it does to William Faulkner. Faulkner's popularity has long since transcended the local readership of the *Double Dealer*, and myriad analyses of his modernist techniques recall Warren's description of fiction that proceeds 'from the inside out.'

Faulkner's works occupy an ambiguous position in North American criticism by straddling the two camps of 'spatial form' and thematic historicism. On the one hand, Faulkner's fiction has provoked more dissertations on 'spatial form' than has that of perhaps any other American author.[3] On the other hand, thematic studies of Faulkner's reference to the specific time and place he describes are equally numerous. What is lacking is an attempt to examine a correlation between the two: an analysis of how his narrative poetics is bound to specificity of time and place.

Faulkner scholarship is divided into two main camps: thematic studies of correlations between his fictional Yoknapatawpha County and the South he lived in, and analytic studies of his linguistic and narrative techniques. The former view his artifice as, at best, a deliberate obfuscation; Conrad Aiken, for example, describes Faulkner's style as 'a calculated system of screens and obtrusions, of confusions and ambiguous interpolations' (136–7). Critics like Aiken – who find it 'annoying, at the end of a sentence, to find that one does not know in the least what was the subject of the verb that dangles *in vacuo*' (139) – usually go on to untangle Faulkner's complicated narratives in order to piece together a unified image of a fictional world that is more in keeping with their own perception of how a world should look. Faulkner himself is at least partly responsible for these earnest attempts to translate his impressionistic prose into realistic images: after all, the author himself gave his fictional world a name, drew maps of it, and formulated complicated genealogies of its inhabitants.

Analyses of Faulkner's narrative technique, if they are concerned at all with his fiction's reference to a historical time and place, dismiss his works' referentiality as coincidental. One critic, for example, goes so far as to suggest that Faulkner merely 'stumbled upon a resourceful literary shorthand – Yoknapatawpha – that was rich enough for his genius (McHaney 59). Critics interested in Faulkner's poetics seem to intuit a correlation between poetics and place, but despite titles containing such promising phrases as 'The Meaning of Form,' 'Style as Vision,' and 'The Meaning of Place,'[4] critics in this camp invariably limit themselves to the third of Mitchell's four strata, the metaphoric 'space' of narrative structure, and ignore the second stratum, the represented world of Faulkner's fiction.

The Agrarians had identified the need for a new means of expressing regional identity, and modernist poetics offered such an alternative. Faulkner devoted most of his literary career to uniting regionalist goals with modernist poetics: his well-documented alternative to realist 'reportage' stems from his lifelong attempt 'from his region [to] confront the total and moving world' (to use Davidson's expression). One of the clearest examples of Faulkner's regionalist alternative to realist poetics is *Go Down, Moses*, a contentious work that has attracted relatively little critical attention except for a heated debate over whether it can even be considered a unified literary work of art.

The confusion over whether or not *Go Down, Moses* can be considered a novel is understandable: several of the book's chapters first appeared in magazines as short stories, and early editions bore the title *Go Down, Moses and Other Stories*. Since 1948, when publishers gave in to Faulkner's demand that 'and Other Stories' be deleted from the title, critics have been reluctant to contradict the author's insistence that *Go Down, Moses* is a unified work. Nevertheless, several critics seem compelled to reduce the work to seven autonomous, paraphrasable stories. In *Threads Cable-Strong*, for example, Dirk Kuyk offers a highly sophisticated argument for unity based on the work's interweaving of complex narrative voices. But Kuyk then uses this analysis of narrative voice as if it were the key to unravelling the tangled 'threads' of seven distinct stories; his summaries of seven 'fabula' are highly detailed plot summaries. Other attempts to account for the novel's unity are more overtly qualified: one critic firmly upholds the conviction that *Go Down, Moses* is a hermetic structure, but only if one of the seven chapters is deleted.[5] Another critic grudgingly accords it the status of a 'loosely constructed novel,' pointing to a hunting theme that makes at least a tenuous appearance in each of the seven chapters.[6]

Faulkner's innate talent for storytelling makes it difficult for the reader to abandon the 'deeply rooted habit' that Bergson describes of extending time into space. Faulkner exploits the reader's natural tendency to look for linear continuity by positing enticing suggestions of narrative coherence throughout *Go Down, Moses*. The novel does contain a paraphrasable core of events, and the untangling of these events poses a challenge for even the most perspicacious reader. If after months, or even years, of arduous labour a critic discovers lacunae, Faulkner's carefully crafted narrative 'threads' lead one to seek explanations, either by describing the work as *almost* a novel, or by applying unified theories of theme or voice to justify gaps in narrative continuity. The work's aesthetic unity, however, resides in a complex interaction not only of plot, theme, and voice, but of the four strata described by Mitchell. This interaction is governed by specificity of time and place, and links human identity to regional specificity.

At the centre of *Go Down, Moses*'s fictional world is a building, a shack that was once a plantation's commissary. In this building is a text, the ledger in which generations of commerce are recorded – not only economic commerce measured in cotton sold and wages paid, but human commerce: the buying and selling of slaves, as well as the births, marriages, and deaths of the plantation's inhabitants. Pages of the fictional ledger are transcribed directly into the text of the chapter entitled 'The Bear,' and as Isaac McCaslin pores over the ledger's contents, readers are given fragmentary glimpses of the 'facts' upon which the other chapters of *Go Down, Moses* are based.

Unlike Presley's journal in *The Octopus*, this text-within-a-text is not an isolated fragment in a minor episode; instead, it reveals not only the narrative content of the rest of the novel, but the thematic import of all those narrated events. The ledger is a record of the characters' attachment to the land; the narrator describes the ledger's accounts as 'threads frail as truth and impalpable as equators yet cable-strong to bind for life them who made the cotton to the land their sweat fell on' (256). As Isaac pores over the tales of miscegenation and incest, of the exploitation of the Indians from whom the land was originally purchased, and of the slaves whose labour is the source of the agrarian economy, he gradually comes to realize that the ledger is more than just the history of one plantation, that 'that chronicle ... was a whole land in miniature, which multiplied and compounded was the entire South' (293).

This *mise-en-abîme* depiction of Faulkner's regionalist intention (to portray 'a whole land in miniature') is more than a thematic passkey. If Faulkner had believed that a plantation ledger could reveal the ties binding Southerners to the South, he could simply have expanded his transcription of the ledger's contents and done away with the novel's narrative complexity. Although regional identity begins with localized topography and climate, regionalism, like literature, is not a natural phenomenon, but a human construct, and the layering of ontological levels in *Go Down, Moses* is part of Faulkner's strategy for mirroring the world-making process involved in forming distinct regional identities.

Not only is the commissary the spatial centre of *Go Down, Moses*'s represented world (the narrator describes it as 'not the heart perhaps but certainly the solar-plexus' of the plantation [255]), but the ledger within the commissary provides a historical centre of the novel's represented world. The scene described in 'The Bear' takes place on Isaac's twenty-first birthday, in October 1888. That moment in 1888, when Isaac realizes that the ledger contains 'a whole land in miniature,' is at the centre of a historical frame whose borders are defined by the end of the Civil War and the abolition of slavery; the moment of Isaac's realization is situated 'twenty-three years after surrender [1865] and twenty-four from emancipation [1912]' (293). This forty-seven-year frame places Isaac at the centre of a specific era: the defeat of the South, twenty-three years earlier, marked the beginning of the end of the South's plantation-based aristocracy; and emancipation, twenty-four years later, would mark the end of the slave empire upon which that society was built. This frame is in turn situated within a larger historical frame encompassing the novel's entire represented world; references in the novel reach back to 1828, when Carothers McCaslin acquired the plantation's land through the Indian Land Patent, and forward to events in 1941. This historical frame covers a span of 113 years, roughly at the centre of which is Isaac's twenty-first birthday. (The exact centre would be 1884, four years prior to Isaac's twenty-first birthday.)

The forward- and backward-reaching temporal references bracketing the incident narrated in 'The Bear' construct a circular chronology that places the character directly in the centre of a world defined by the simultaneous influences of the region's past and future. A similar pattern can be found in a sentence structure that recurs throughout *Go Down, Moses*; Bruce Southard has observed that the novel's language is characterized by 'centre-embedded constructions,' as opposed to the more traditional 'right-branching constructions.' Southard does not relate this sentence structure to the broader issue of thematic meaning, but within a theory of regionalism, Southard's observation illustrates how sentence syntax can contribute to the construction of a distinct kind of fictional world. In *Go Down, Moses*, Faulkner manipulates traditional English syntax in order to create a 'centre-embedded' world, one that is pieced together from the inside out through the perceiving consciousness of its inhabitants.

One example of Faulkner's unconventional sentence structure can be found in 'The Old People' in a paragraph taking up almost an entire page and comprising a single sentence. The sentence begins with a simple statement: 'They were the white boy, marked forever, and the old dark man sired on both sides by savage kings' (165). What follows is a string of modifiers, alternating in reference between the boy and the man. The following excerpt illustrates the passage's pattern of alternating 'centre-embedded' modifiers: 'The man would continue to live past the boy's seventy years and then eighty years, long after the man himself had entered the earth as chiefs and kings entered it; – the child, not yet a man, whose grandfather had lived in the same country and in almost the same manner as the boy himself would grow up to live, leaving his descendants in the land in his turn as his grandfather had done' (165). The passage ends with a reference to the man's (Sam Fathers's) Indian blood 'drawing toward the end of its alien and irrevocable course, barren, since Sam Fathers had no children' (165). The string of modifiers in this passage reaches back in history to the 'savage kings' of Sam's ancestry, and projects forward to Isaac's descendants. The sentence's syntax, however, resists situating the narrative present within any sequential (or 'right-branching') chronology. Isaac McCaslin is once again inextricably linked to the region's past and future: at the centre of the sentence's elusive temporality, Isaac is tied to the land by the region's Indian heritage and by his own destiny to continue that heritage.

Another example of this 'centre-embedded' syntax can be found in the novel's opening passage, which purportedly introduces the subject of the single chapter, but in fact foreshadows the regionalist project that informs the whole novel: 'this was not something participated in or even seen by himself, but by his elder cousin, McCaslin Edmonds, grandson of Isaac's father's sister and so descended by the distaff, yet notwithstanding the inheritor, and in his time the bequestor, of that which some had thought then and some still thought should have been Isaac's, since his was the name in which the title to the land had first been granted from the Indian patent and which some of the descendants of his father's slaves still bore in the land' (3). Like the previous example from 'The Bear,' this passage reaches forward and backward to the temporal borders of the region's history within a syntax that resists causal closure (the 'sentence' also ignores the orthographic conventions of capital letter and period).

And once again the rapid-fire juxtaposition of forward- and backward-leaping historical references links the character's identity to the interpenetrating influences of the region's past and future. In this instance, Isaac is bound to the land by the complicated rules of patriarchal inheritance inscribed in the region's agrarian culture.

Critics who seek justification for Faulkner's insistence that *Go Down, Moses* is a unified work often refer to thematic unity, and the prevailing conclusion is that all but one of the narrated episodes contribute to a unified whole. Cleanth Brooks set the precedent when he identified the McCaslin family history as the novel's unifying thread, and concluded that since 'Pantaloon in Black' does not contribute to this family history, 'it may be that Faulkner decided to include it in this book only because it reveals one more aspect of the world in which "The Bear" takes place' (257). Brooks's assessment of 'Pantaloon' triggered a succession of attempts to contradict him by finding evidence of unifying themes in 'Pantaloon,' as well as accompanying counter-arguments in support of Brooks. For example, Olga Vickery grudgingly supports Brooks's thematic-unity argument, but feels compelled to qualify her inclusion of 'Pantaloon,' because the hunting theme she identifies as the novel's unifying thread makes only a tenuous appearance in this chapter. Stanley Tick takes a contrary position, faulting Vickery for even attempting to include 'Pantaloon' in her argument for unity. Tick echoes Brooks with his conclusion that '"Pantaloon" must be considered the unintegrated and therefore non-essential part of the [novel's] structure' (329).

'Pantaloon' can be incorporated with the rest of the novel if it is placed in the context of the regionalist intention suggested by the ledger in 'The Bear.' Brooks notes in passing that despite its exclusion from the McCaslin history, 'Pantaloon' is linked to at least part of the rest of the novel by its reference to a fire in Rider's hearth on his wedding night similar to the fire in Lucas Beauchamp's hearth described in 'The Fire and the Hearth.' Intent on proving his thesis about a unifying family history, Brooks dismisses the recurrence of this 'primitive-man' sub-theme as coincidental. But if regionalism accounts for the unity in *Go Down, Moses*, this theme explains Rider's response to the world around him, and the narration of the theme serves the same structural function as the ledger in 'The Bear' and Faulkner's innovative syntax throughout the novel: it is a *mise-en-abîme* depiction of the mapping of borders that isolate a distinct, regional world from the broader world that surrounds it.

'Pantaloon' illustrates a Faulknerian technique that critics allude to in their references to 'voice' and 'point of view.'[7] The story's plot centres on Rider, and the events are narrated through various internal focalizations. These focalizations indicate that Rider's actions are incomprehensible to those around him – to his co-workers, to his aunt, and to the sheriff's deputy. The sections that are filtered through Rider's consciousness occur well into the story, after Rider has downed most of a jug of liquor. As these passages are filtered through Rider's numbed senses, the world seems to come to a standstill: when he lopes across the moonlit countryside, we are given the eerily still image of 'his motionless shadow and that of the lifted jug slanting across the slope' (148). When he enters the sawmill yard, the site of frantic activity earlier that day, Rider discovers a stillness and a kind of peace: he stands, 'blinking about at the stacked lumber, the skidway, the piled logs waiting for tomorrow, the boiler-shed all quiet and blanched in the moon. And then it was all right' (151).

Like the ledger at the centre of the novel – a unified narrative that accounts for the chaotic narrative fragments in the chapters surrounding it – or like Isaac, the perceiving subject at the centre of a sentence's temporal short-circuits, Rider in this scene becomes the still centre of a chaotic world as he attempts to find meaning in the events around him. Those events attest to an agrarian world gone mad: whites cheat blacks at dice, blacks murder whites; blacks turn against their own kind. The 'primitive' world that makes its appearance here is an agrarian world that is at odds with the industrial world of the contemporary South. Rider clings to a world defined by simple agrarian values, a world in which whites are masters, blacks are slaves, and relations between the two are held in a tenuous balance by the niceties of social protocol. This is the same world attested to by the contents of the ledger, the same world that Isaac finds himself at the centre of during his initiation rite with Sam Fathers. This is the world that the entire novel maps out: provisional, defined by regional history and culture, a marginal world that is being assaulted by external forces, forces that finally transgress regional borders, thereby erasing differences and co-opting the region into a larger unity.

The spatial and temporal centres of *Go Down, Moses*'s represented world are thematic: the commissary scene defines a central point within the represented world of the characters, or on the third of Mitchell's four strata. This thematic centring is duplicated by a centring on the other levels of Mitchell's model: the scene is more or less central in the physical positioning of the novel's chapters; the October afternoon on which Isaac McCaslin repudiates his patriarchal heritage provides a centre for the 'interpenetration' of past and present evident on the sentence level and on the larger level of narrative structure; and Isaac's revelation imparts significance, or meaning, to the narrative fragments scattered throughout the rest of the novel. Although it disrupts linear causality, *Go Down, Moses* does not deny formal closure; it merely presents an alternative to the linear form of realist narrative. The region is still portrayed as an identifiable object, and an understanding of regional identity is implicitly linked to the construction of an autonomous aesthetic object. Regional identity and aesthetic autonomy are not imposed from the perspective of external authority, but are pieced together 'from the inside out' (Warren, *Southern Harvest* xvi). Specificity of real-world time and place are just as essential for Faulkner as they were for Cunha or Norris; the difference between realist and modernist narrative poetics merely means that specificity of time and place provide an internal centre rather than an external frame.

THE CANADIAN PRAIRIE: SINCLAIR ROSS'S *AS FOR ME AND MY HOUSE*

Like their U.S. counterparts in the previous century, early twentieth-century Canadian prairie writers saw their surrounding environment as a vast emptiness. Tracing the origins of Canadian prairie fiction, Dick Harrison describes what early settlers saw all around them as an emptiness so vast it defied naming (1–44). Prairie settlers responded by trying to force the foreign environment to conform to their familiar frames of reference, with little success: sidewalks sank into oceans of prairie mud; spats and leather shoes were splattered with that mud; and parasols and silk dresses were shredded by the prairie wind. Early literary attempts to domesticate the prairie were similarly fruitless as writers tried to force the unknown country into familiar literary forms. Writing about half a century later than their U.S. counterparts, the pioneers of Canadian prairie fiction found themselves struggling to frame the prairie experience within realist frames of reference, rather than the romantic forms that had guided early U.S. regionalism. One of the most prolific early prairie regionalists was Frederick Philip Grove, and his fiction illustrates not only the realist approach to domesticating the environment through naming, but also the naturalist tendency to seek determinist explanations for regional identity.

Like many of Canada's early prairie writers, Grove was himself a settler, and just as he staked his claim on the prairie by erecting fences and 'cultivating' the soil, so in his novels Grove shaped prairie reality according to the pre-determined forms of European models. Grove's regionalism was guided by his view of the prairie as a unique manifestation of universal laws: he saw in prairie existence 'a new or distinctive shade of the generally tragic reaction of human souls to the fundamental conditions of man's life on earth,' and his literary ambition was to chronicle that distinctive prairie 'shade' (*It Needs to Be Said* 155). The plots of Grove's novels are determined by a prairie code of survival: stake a claim, cultivate the land, and perpetuate the claim through marriage and procreation. In *Settlers of the Marsh,* for example, the 'generally tragic reaction of human souls' is given its 'distinctive shade' when Mrs. Vogel, the protagonist Niels's targeted matriarch, refuses to provide him with the required offspring; this breach of prairie law drives Niels to a frenzy that culminates in his wife's murder. Grove's *Our Daily Bread* provides another example of his vision of the prairie's distinctive influence on humanity: the protagonist's tragic demise begins when his offspring refuse to remain within the borders of the homestead, but instead 'look to the externals' of city life (*Settlers of the Marsh* 81).

Early prairie fiction framed the settlers' experience in homesteading narratives that portray a claim's fences as borders guarding the internal unity and order of the homestead against the external lawlessness of the Canadian prairie. In more recent prairie fiction, the vast emptiness envisioned by early settlers and writers has provided a ground for the dramatization of an existential conflict pitting the internal unity of human consciousness against the horrifying void of an unknowable external world. Heidegger's *Being and Time* provides a description of this existential 'nothingness' that aptly describes the early-twentieth-century perceptions of the prairie. Heidegger refers to an emptiness that is a constant source of anxiety because it threatens our identity, yet we are unable to confront that emptiness and give it a name: 'That in the face of which one has anxiety is characterized by the fact that what threatens is *nowhere* ... That which threatens cannot bring itself close from a definite direction within what is close by; it is already "there," and yet nowhere; it is so close that it is oppressive and stifles one's breath, and yet it is nowhere' (186). This description of a terrifying nothingness could almost serve as a dust-jacket synopsis of a landmark Canadian prairie novel: Sinclair Ross's *As for Me and My House.* In this novel Ross confronts the void that is as much a part of prairie identity as the homesteads and towns settlers erected in an attempt to keep that void at bay.

As for Me and My House is a story about fleeing this nothingness, and the fleeing is portrayed as a futile attempt to keep that nothingness at bay through artificial social conventions. Ross's prairie town is an updated

version of Grove's homestead: the fences that for Grove had contained
the forces of social order are replaced in *As for Me and My House* by the
parameters of a small Canadian prairie town in the 1930s. Ross, however,
reverses the perspective on these borders. By narrating the novel in the
first person through Mrs Bentley, the wife of an itinerant preacher, Ross
gives the view not of the colonizing patriarch, but of his unwitting accomplice. The novel portrays a conflict between husband and wife, and as the
protagonist burrows ever deeper into worlds of his own making, his wife
gradually recognizes her complicity in the building of the barriers that
alienate the region's inhabitants from the land they occupy.

As for Me and My House is narrated entirely by Mrs Bentley in the form
of diary entries, and the world that emerges through these entries is
claustrophobic. The walls of the house stifle the inhabitants, not because
they isolate those inside from the exterior world, but because the world
outside constantly seeps in – through the doors and windows, through
cracks in the walls, and through the roof – only to remind the occupants
of the prison that they have built for themselves. In the middle of a
prairie summer, when Philip locks himself away in his study and Mrs
Bentley busies herself in the kitchen, the heat inside the house is
described as 'heavy and suffocating'; Mrs Bentley imagines that she and
her husband are 'embedded in it, like insects in a fluid that had con-
gealed' (117). The howling wind outside makes the walls seem all the
more fragile: 'The wind poured by, and we were immersed and lost in it.
I sat breathing from my throat, my muscles tense. To relax, I felt, would
be to let the walls around me crumple in' (38). In the summer, dust
seeps in through cracks in the walls, spreading a fine film over everything, from the food the Bentleys eat to the sheets they sleep in. In
winter, as snow piles up outside, frost collects inside; Mrs Bentley wakes
to find every metal surface in the kitchen coated in ice. During the spring
rains, as Mrs Bentley lies in bed listening to water dripping in, 'the walls
seemed to press closer, driven in by the night and the wetness' (118).

Although she is the narrator, Mrs Bentley is not the protagonist, but
the follower. As Philip moves from one isolated prairie outpost to
another, she tags along, constantly hoping to break down the walls of his
isolation. (As if to reinforce her role as follower, Ross identifies her
throughout only as Mrs Bentley; we are never given her first name.)
Philip's life is dedicated to fleeing the prairie, and his dream of escape
begins in his childhood: 'He grew up in one of these little Main Streets,
rebelling against its cramp and pettiness, looking farther. Somewhere,
potential, unknown, there was another world, his world; and every day the

train sped into it, and every day he watched it, hungered, went on dreaming' (29). But when he follows those train tracks (with his wife in tow), Philip finds only an endless prairie. When they settle for a few years in one of the towns that dot the prairie landscape, the town is aptly named Horizon. Mrs Bentley reflects gloomily on her prospects: 'another Horizon every three or four years – that's not much of a prospect to look forward to' (156).

In Horizon, Philip turns inward in his attempt to find a refuge from the emptiness of the prairie; he barricades himself in his study and turns to art. First, he tries his hand at writing a novel, but the world of his fiction is no less stifling than the world of Horizon: as Mrs Bentley explains, 'His book was a failure. The little world that it had meant for him collapsed' (64). He then tries painting, and meets with limited success; through Mrs. Bentley, we get a running commentary throughout the novel on Philip's artistic progress. One painting Mrs Bentley admires depicts horses freezing in a blizzard: 'The way the poor brutes stand with their hindquarters huddled up and their heads thrust over the wire, the tug and swirl of the blizzard, the fence lost in it, only a post or two away – a good job, if it's good in a picture to make you feel terror and pity and desolation' (153). In another passage, Mrs Bentley admires a painting in which Philip portrays the town of Horizon: 'The town is seen from a distance, a lost little clutter on the long sweep of prairie. High above it dust clouds wheel and wrestle heedlessly. Here, too, wind is master' (74). Despite what Mrs Bentley sees as flashes of brilliance, Philip becomes increasingly frustrated, and we learn that ultimately his attempts to capture the region on canvas are a failure: 'Something has happened to his drawing, and something has happened to him. There have always been Horizons – he was born and grew up in one – but once they were a challenge. Their pettiness and cramp stung him to defiance, made him reach farther. Now in his attitude there's still defiance, but it's a sullen, hopeless kind. These little towns threaten to be the scaffolding of his life, and at last he seems to know' (17).

In a telling commentary on one of Philip's paintings, Mrs Bentley identifies the source of the oppressive atmosphere that pervades her world. She praises Phillip's depiction of an old horse: 'A broken old horse, legs set stolid, head down dull and spent. But still you feel it belongs to the earth, the earth it stands on, the prairie that continues where the town breaks off' (69). Where the painting fails, according to Mrs Bentley, is in its depiction of the town in which the old horse and buggy are situated: 'But the town in contrast has an upstart, mean complacency. The false fronts haven't seen the prairie. Instead they stare at each other across the street as into mirrors of themselves, absorbed in their own reflections' (69). Mrs Bentley concludes her criticism with a decisive pronouncement: 'The town shouldn't be there' (69). While Philip fiddles with the painting, 'giving last little touches here and there, as if it were just a matter of perspective, or a rounder buggy wheel' (69), Mrs Bentley can hardly restrain the urge to reach over Philip's shoulder 'to smudge it out and let the underlying rhythms complete themselves' (69).

The simple statement 'The town shouldn't be there' could be a fitting conclusion to Ross's novel, the moral of his story. The novel's oppressive atmosphere emanates not from the region itself, but from the artificial barriers that the region's inhabitants have built between themselves and the land they inhabit. These barriers are tangible in the walls of Mrs Bentley's house and in the 'huddled little cluster of houses and stores' (59) that constitute the town of Horizon. Ross also depicts the intangible social barriers that have evolved from the patriarchal imperatives of the traditional settlement narratives. The lives of Horizon's inhabitants are dominated by the same social order that guided Grove's characters: stake out borders (in this case, of a town rather than a farm), and then 'prove' the claim by 'cultivating' the land (in this case, by erecting false-fronted buildings). Mrs Bentley's world is dominated by the stifling conventions of a small-town society that has evolved from these founding principles.

Ross's *mise-en-abîme* depiction of Philip as a failed regionalist is similar to Norris's depiction of Presley, but *As for Me and My House* differs from *The Octopus* in one crucial aspect: the frustrated regionalist is not described from the perspective of an omniscient narrator who situates the characters in a broader context. The source of Philip's failure is identified not by an omniscient narrator, but by Mrs Bentley, who, through the pages of her diary, completes the regionalist project that eluded her husband. By abandoning the convention of the omniscient narrator, Ross succeeds where Norris had failed: the represented world of *As for Me and My House* is not a 'mere segment' of a 'full round,' but an autonomous world defined entirely by local forces. Ross uses irony where earlier regionalists had relied on didacticism; he recreates in his fiction the hermetic world of small-town prairie life, while at the same time demonstrating the futility of attempting to contain the prairie within such artificial borders.

THE DOUBLE HOOK

In 1935 Sheila Watson moved from Vancouver to Dog Creek, a remote community in the interior of British Columbia, where she would live for two years. Living in Toronto some fifteen years later, she drew on that experience when she sat down to write *The Double Hook*, which was finally published in 1959. In the nearly twenty-five years that intervened between raw impressions and a polished final draft of a novel, narrative poetics underwent considerable re-evaluation and innovation, and inconsistencies between Watson's stated intentions and her completed novel have been a source of confusion for literary critics.

As Sherrill Grace points out, Watson's fascination with modernism was evident in the course work she completed at the University of British Columbia prior to her taking up a teaching post in Dog Creek, and it continued long past her stay in British Columbia's interior and resulted in her 1956 doctoral thesis entitled 'Wyndham Lewis and Expressionism.' Grace responds to a long-neglected gap in critical studies of *The Double Hook* by focusing on Watson's poetics, and astutely observes that Watson's familiarity with expressionism is clearly evident in *The Double Hook*. Grace's conclusions, however, illustrate some obvious contradictions in common perceptions of regionalism. For example, there is no hint of irony in the detailed account of British Columbia geography with which Grace prefaces her study of *The Double Hook* – a study intent on proving that Watson's novel is entirely divorced from geographic specificity.

Watson said that she did not intend to write a 'western,' and declared that *The Double Hook* was not a regional novel.[8] She is absolutely right, but only if 'regionalism' is meant in the limited sense of descriptive realism. *The Double Hook* is a slender volume with only sparse descriptions of setting, and certainly bears little resemblance to such voluminous catalogues of local detail as Norris's *The Octopus* and Grove's prairie novels. Watson clearly did not, however, imply a rejection of regionalism in the sense of writing about the effect of specificity of place on human identity. Watson describes herself as 'very provincial, very local, very much a part of [her] own milieu' ('What I'm Going to Do' 14), and states explicitly that her purpose was to write about a particular place. She qualifies her statement by adding that she had intended to disprove the belief that one could not write about a specific place in Canada without ending up 'with a regional novel of some kind' ('What I'm Going to Do' 14). This qualification clearly was a rejection not of regionalism per se, but only of the kind of local-colour realism that was being rejected at the same time by Freyre and his colleagues in Brazil, and by the Agrarians and Faulkner in the United States.

Critics nevertheless interpret Watson's reference to regionalism as a blanket rejection of specificity of time and place in fiction. Grace has no reservations about declaring that 'what [Watson] finally wrote did not mirror external reality – British Columbia Cariboo country' (186), or about claiming that despite language's inherent and inevitable referentiality, 'Watson has achieved a remarkable degree of resistance to representation' (192). Such claims proceed from the unquestioned assumption that referentiality is synonymous with realist techniques, an assumption which in turn leads to the conclusion that a non-realist work like *The Double Hook* cannot be regionalist. Watson herself is ambivalent about *The Double Hook*'s intended referentiality, saying that she 'wanted to do something about the West, which wasn't a Western; and about Indians which wasn't about ... Indians' ('What I'm Going to Do' 14). Critics often cite this statement as proof that Watson intended to deny real-world representation, but the ambiguous statement could just as easily be cited as proof that Watson *did* intend to write about the West and about Indians.

A confirmation of the novel's referentiality can be found in the author's description of characters in her novel as 'figures in a ground, from which they could not be separated' ('What I'm Going to Do' 15). The statement makes an obvious allusion to Jamesian aesthetic unity, and it is often mistakenly cited as proof of Watson's perception of literature as an abstract unity divorced from real-world specifics. Grace, for example, cites a passage from Wyndham Lewis (which Watson quotes in her doctoral thesis) about transforming the essential 'shaping power' of life's 'vibrations' into abstract aesthetic forms. Grace refers to Watson's familiarity with Lewis in support of her contention that by referring to characters in *The Double Hook* as 'figures in a ground,' Watson was referring to an abstract unity in which 'human beings are figures in a ground, patterns in time and space' (194). But it was not a generalized passion for 'human beings in time and space' that motivated Watson; she specifies that what she had in mind was not an abstract aesthetic ground, but a very specific 'ground' in the literal sense. Watson explains that she wanted to write a novel in which 'people are entwined in, they're interacting with the landscape, and the landscape is interacting with them' ('What I'm Going to Do,' 15). Watson qualifies her reference to landscape, adding that the characters in her novel interact with more than just the landscape: 'Not the landscape, the things about them, the other things which exist' ('What I'm Going to Do,' 15). Her semantic faltering has a now-familiar sound: the nebulous 'things' for which she cannot find a name are similar to the horrifying shapes that confronted Norris's character when he sat down to compose a regionalist poem; describing their attempts to capture this 'mystery of place' confounded many regionalist authors.

Watson's reference to 'ground' may very well have been a deliberately ambiguous reference to both external landscape and internal aesthetic form, but if so, the representational half of this two-sided reference is consistently ignored by critics. Critics also ignore, or are simply blind to, similar ambiguities that riddle both Watson's stated intentions and her novel. With regard to representation, it is true that Watson did not want to write a regional novel, but she *did* want to write something provincial and local, something that would reflect her experience of living in the Cariboo in the 1930s. And as for thematic unity, Watson does refer to art, tradition, and ritual in one breath as the unifying forces of human civilization;[9] yet, as we shall see, there are contradictory regional forces at work in *The Double Hook*.

Recognizing the evidence contradicting the prevailing theory that *The Double Hook* is a non-regional abstraction requires a careful distinction between syntactic structure and linguistic reference. On the level of syntax, both in sentence structure and in emplotment, Watson's prose exhibits signs of the modernist tendency towards aesthetic abstraction. But on the denotative level of reference, Watson 'grounds' this stylistic experimentation in a very specific time and place. If we consider the fourth of W.J.T. Mitchell's strata of 'spatial form' – 'the metaphysics which lies behind a story told about *this* world in *this* particular way' – we will see that in *The Double Hook* syntax and reference combine to create a distinct reality, one governed by forces indigenous to the region.

Watson's sentences are for the most part short and are often fragmentary. The effect can be to mimic the simultaneity of sensory perception, as in a description focalized through the Widow: 'All around the animals waited. The plate on the table. The knife. The fork. The kettle boiling on the stove' (55). Watson occasionally applies these fragmentary sentences to the Proustian technique of narrating through a mediating consciousness in which past and present merge in sensory perception and the memory it evokes: 'The remembrance of event and the slash of rain merged. Time annihilated in the concurrence. The present contracted into the sweet hot cup he fondled. Vast fingers circling it' (39). Such interpenetration of past and present is rare in *The Double Hook*. Whereas Proust uses the technique to frame a complicated series of flashbacks within an instantaneous recollection triggered in a character, Felix's moment of introspection in *The Double Hook* is an isolated experiment within a narrative that for the most part follows a diachronic sequence of events.

On the level of narrative syntax, Watson's juxtaposition of fragmentary sentences is frequently similar to Faulkner's technique of creating the illusion of static motion. The narration of an event in the novel's opening passage, for example, resembles Faulkner's description of the deer, both 'still' and 'forever leaping':

James was at the top of the stairs. His hand half-raised. His voice in the rafters.

James walking away. The old lady falling. There under the jaw of the roof. In the vault of the bed loft. Into the shadow of death. (19)

The effect of this passage is the prose equivalent of the effect of expressionist painting: as in Duchamps's 'Nude Descending a Staircase,' descent is implied through images of frozen movement. In this passage movement is frozen in the eternal present of the present participle, and images are run together through the juxtaposition of incomplete sentences. Whereas for Faulkner the juxtaposition of isolated moments is a structuring principle extending beyond the sentence level to the entire narrative organization of *Go Down, Moses*, in *The Double Hook* this technique is limited to a few isolated passages.

On the level of reference, *The Double Hook* exhibits a more pervasive technique that involves not temporal, but spatial interpenetration. We have seen one example, the juxtaposition of external and internal spatial references in the kitchen description cited above, wherein an external reference – 'All around the animals waited' – is followed immediately by a string of fragmentary internal references: 'The plate on the table. The knife. The fork ...' Internal/external spatial juxtaposition is extended over a longer passage in the following example:

James opened the door again. This time to look out.

You'd best put your beast in, he said. The far stall's empty.

The boy walked towards the steps.

I'm not stopping, he said.

You'd best come in, James said, till it blows over.

What I've come about won't blow over, said the boy.

Then you'd best go away with it, James said.

The boy saw the door closing. He jumped the steps and caught at the handle, pulling the door open into the wind. (45)

The rapid juxtaposition of these paired oppositions – opening the door

102 New World Regionalism

to look out; inviting the boy to come in, then to go away; the door closing, the door opening – creates an unstable ground, a spatial flux comparable to the temporal flux of Faulkner's *Go Down, Moses.*

We can find further evidence of this internal/external opposition in Watson's distinctive use of narrative voice. As the passage cited above shows, Watson does not use quotation marks to identify represented speech. This lack of punctuation, together with rapid switching of focalization, has the effect of blurring the boundary between the narrator and the narration, between the internal world of the characters and the external world of narrative authority. We can see the effect of this technique in a passage beginning with a nonfocalized description in the voice of an external narrator: 'They had reached the line fence now. The house was still hidden by the sweep of the land' (83). The narration then switches to a focalized description, narrated as direct speech: 'Lenchen's gone from home, the boy said.' Two focalized descriptions follow, one presented as direct speech, the other in the voice of the narrator: 'There's no smoke coming from the chimney, he said to Ara as they rounded the bend. She looked. The road reached before them to the gate, which hung open on its hinges' (83). This is followed by a short paragraph in which the narration switches rapidly between three focalizations, all in the narrator's voice: 'William leant down from his saddle and looked at the marks in the dust. Ara smelt the scent of the honeysuckle. But the boy saw a head at the window half screened by the vine' (83). The passage concludes with focalized direct speech, nonfocalized narrative voice, and focalized direct speech in rapid succession: 'There's someone there, he said. William looked up from the dust. It's Greta, he said, but James must have gone off somewhere, leaving the gate open behind him' (83). Although each of the transitions in focalization and voice is marked by speech tags or similar indications of shifts in focalization ('She looked,' 'William leant ... and looked,' 'Ara smelt,' 'the boy saw'), the rapid switch of focalization and voice, not signalled by quotation marks in the text, blurs ontological borders between narrator and narrated.

Watson's distinctive style of short, often fragmentary sentences extends from sentence syntax to narrative syntax, or emplotment. The book is divided into five sections, each of which contains about a dozen short narrative segments. These segments typically begin by positing a character's point of view, and follow with a brief scene narrated through that focalizing consciousness. For example, the segments in the opening chapter begin by introducing a scene through the vision of a character:

'Ara saw her fishing along the creek' (3), 'Felix saw the old lady' (4), 'The Widow's boy saw the old lady' (5), 'From the kitchen window, the Widow looked out to the hills' (8), 'Lenchen watched her mother walk away' (9). Each brief segment that follows these opening focal orientations corresponds to the Bergsonian notion of 'facts of consciousness.' Juxtaposing these segments, however, creates not a contradictory tension of past and present, as in Faulkner, but an interpenetration of places. Each segment is not only focalized through a perceiving consciousness, but tied to a place; most often, scenes are focalized from within or near one of the five houses that dot the fictional landscape. The effect of this spatial orientation is to associate characters' identities with specific places, and the juxtaposition of the brief focalized segments creates an interpenetration that is more spatial than temporal.

The five larger narrative segments, or chapters, group events in a pattern similar to that of the five acts of Shakespearean drama, and the result is a drama of place. The first chapter introduces the characters and setting: there are twelve characters, and except for Angel Prosper, who has left her husband to live with Theophil, all are paired with their proper families and live in their own houses. In the second chapter this comfortable world is shaken up: families are divided and tentative new alliances are formed. The conflict reaches its climax in the third chapter: spouses and siblings set out to retrieve errant family members, and the chapter closes with the Potter house going up in flames, taking Greta to her death. The fourth chapter is an interlude: while the conflict awaits resolution, the narration follows a single character who leaves the setting and contemplates the state of affairs from afar. The fifth chapter is the denouement, in which lovers are reunited with loved ones.

There are numerous parallels between *The Double Hook* and stories from European mythology, stories of sin and redemption, or of the questing hero returning to home and family.[10] Watson clearly employs the familiar modernist technique of using myth to impart order to an unordered universe, but there is more than one mythology at work in *The Double Hook*. In addition to familiar biblical and classical myths, *The Double Hook* incorporates an indigenous, local myth. The novel opens with an overview of the region and its inhabitants, focalized through Coyote, a figure from Salishan Indian legend: 'In the folds of the hills under Coyote's eye lived [the novel's twelve characters]' (19), and it closes with Coyote's comment on the birth of Lenchen's baby: 'I have set his feet on soft ground; I have set his feet on the sloping shoulders of the world' (134).

The fictional world of *The Double Hook* is not overseen by a single, unifying mythology, but is the site of confrontation between European and indigenous North American mythologies, a confrontation unresolved at the novel's conclusion. Coyote is not an omniscient source of unity, but an alien god, a troublemaker, and a trickster. While the birth at the novel's conclusion is rife with Christian and classical allusions – Grace compares the concluding scene to the nativity, to the redemption, and to the return of the questing hero[11] – it does not represent the triumph of order. Coyote has sown confusion and terror throughout the novel, and this indigenous god's overseeing presence is every bit as evident at the novel's close as in the introductory passage. The characters' fates are determined by a force inextricably linked to the region, a force that they do not understand.

The climactic scene in the third chapter presents the familiar regional topoi of a house that symbolizes identity and internal unity and of a character who, facing the loss of identity, goes mad. But the terror outside the house is not the terror of an alien world beyond regional borders: it is the region itself. *The Double Hook* does not express 'an entire civilization's *Angst*,' as Grace suggests (186), but instead identifies a specific place as the source of a very particular *angst*.

In *The Double Hook* characters confront a region that resists colonization, and this resistance is reflected in a poetics that defies sedimented ontologies. Watson speaks of art and tradition as one side of the double hook, opposed by violence and insensibility on the other side, and critics assume that *The Double Hook* is Watson's offering of an ordering unity. The duality in *The Double Hook*, however, goes much deeper than the order-versus-chaos dichotomy that the author herself describes. Characters and readers alike find traces of comforting narratives in *The Double Hook*, but these are only one half of the double hook. On the other side are opposing forces of difference, and the tension between the two forces is not resolved. Watson's use of indigenous myth, combined with the conscious exploitation of non-traditional linguistic and narrative syntax, foreshadows some of the ways in which postmodern regionalists might use a geographic region as a ground from which to contest Old World hegemony.

CHAPTER FIVE

Multiple Worlds

The regionalist examples we have looked at so far represent varying attitudes towards what D.S. Maxwell has described as the 'act of imaginative adjustment to new surroundings' that all postcolonial authors undertake (84). For romantics, New World regions were a vehicle through which New World culture could find its rightful place in Western civilization. Realists tried to deny the 'gaps, absences, and silences produced by the colonial encounter' that Slemon describes (16) by wielding the world-making power of narrative fiction. Modernists confronted those gaps to portray the existential despair of inhabiting the 'world apart' that Bolívar had first described in his 1815 'Carta de Jamaica.' Postmodern poetics offers a means of exploring a 'middle ground' somewhere between romantic abstraction and naive realism,[1] and some contemporary authors have applied these techniques to regionalist fiction.

The perception of a physical region as 'the site of loss' (Barthes 7), or as the absence of presence, requires a reversal of epistemological assumptions even more radical than modernism's reversal of nineteenth-century positivism. William Spanos suggests that modernism's introspective gaze only perpetuated attempts to disengage critical enquiry from the flux of historical change,[2] and defines postmodern fiction by its rejection of any such claims to temporal disengagement. For Spanos, postmodernism means recognizing one's historicity and attempting to retrieve temporality, which he defines as 'the differences time disseminates' (*Repetitions* 6). To the postmodernist regionalist, regional identity is neither a transcendent symbol, nor a fixed entity, nor an abstract structure defined by subjective patterns of coherence; it is 'in the midst' of this temporal difference.[3]

Spanos's recognition of historicity as the source of difference is drawn from Heidegger's idea of ontological 'destruction.' For Heidegger the history of intellectual enquiry is a perpetual covering-up of authentic being: with each new attempt at explaining man's relation to the world, 'that which remains *hidden* in an egregious sense, or which relapses and gets *covered up* again, or which shows itself only "*in disguise*", is not just this entity or that, but rather the *Being* of entities' (35; Heidegger's emphasis). Heidegger's 'destruction' aims for a dis-covering of authentic being. Spanos designates this kind of ontological destruction as the legitimate aim of postmodern literature, and explains that such literature is 'referential' in that it 'speaks to the de-centered occasion of contemporary men and women' (*Repetitions* 255). Postmodern regionalism, however, not only must reflect historicity in the Heideggerian sense of *Dasein* (being there), but must also locate 'being' in a very specific 'there.' In postmodern regionalist fiction, specificity of place will define a distinctive mode of being, which it is the author's task to dis-cover.

Brian McHale describes some strategies through which postmodern fiction uses real-world places as a means of subverting ontological certainty. For McHale, modernist fiction's metaphoric 'worlds,' which embrace 'epistemological, psychological, or sociological meaning' within a single unifying world (79), did not inherently defy the one-world ontology underlying traditional modes of representation.

McHale explains that in modernist fiction walls or windows frequently serve as metaphoric borders defining self-contained 'life-worlds' (79). We have seen examples of such metaphoric borders in the window through which Dagoberto Marçau gazed out at the Brazilian *sertão* in *A bagaceira*, in the walls containing the surreal world of José Amarro's torment in *Fogo morto*, and in the walls of the McCaslin commissary in *Go Down, Moses*, which that contained 'a whole land in miniature' (293). McHale explains that postmodern fiction no longer portrays these 'worlds' as embedded in a single, unifying ontology, but presents conflicting, contradictory realities. Postmodern fiction, as McHale defines it, portrays the borders separating these worlds as permeable: 'The confrontation between worlds is no longer a psychological and epistemological metaphor, but a literal ontological structure, a fantastic double ontology ... The ontological barrier ultimately fails to keep incommensurable orders of being separate: there is an exchange of identities' (80).

McHale describes the postmodern technique of defying traditional ontological borders through the juxtaposition in fiction of incompatible real-world places. He gives such examples from postmodern fiction as a round-trip train journey from France to Italy, with a stop in Atlanta, Georgia; and the juxtaposition of Toledo, Ohio and Toledo, Spain through references to both Andrew Jackson and Marcus Flavius as founding fathers of a single Toledo.[4] These examples indicate the ways in which postmodern fiction can use real-world referents to subvert the ontological certainty inherent in traditional realist representation; regionalist fiction, however, can draw on only one real-world place as a referent, and this real-world region must provide the 'site' of Barthes's 'seam' or 'cut.' To the postmodern regionalist, a region is neither an external fact nor an internal intentional object; instead, it occupies the void between intent and reality, between book and world.

GONE INDIAN

A group of authors and critics in Western Canada have responded to the challenge of postmodern regionalism by arguing not only that their region has a distinct identity, but that its representation demands a distinctive poetics. Eli Mandel observes that 'so long as the question of distinctiveness in regional writing is not seriously raised, one can be certain that the art itself is thought to be minor, trivial, superficial ... But the moment it is felt to be central, not peripheral, one can be certain the writing itself has assumed a particular character' (107). The distinctive poetics that Mandel proposes stems from recognizing regionalism's inherent preoccupation with borders. As Mandel points out, 'a region is defined by its boundaries, regionalism consisting in the mapping of boundaries – the line between here and there, its distinctiveness' (112). The kind of border that Mandel describes is a paradoxical entity: neither 'here' nor 'there,' it is a hypothetical line, and although it defies quantitative measurement, its presence is undeniable. Mandel astutely observes that 'it is a peculiar art to be able to discern boundaries, borderlines, and to be able to map them in words and images requires great literary tact' (112). By making regionalism's borders – those paradoxical middle grounds – its referent, postmodern regionalism can link the kind of ontological plurality that McHale describes to the representation of a distinct regional identity.

Robert Kroetsch describes the Canadian prairie not as a repository of regional artefacts waiting to be catalogued, but as 'a ground from which to deconstruct' (Miki 88). Kroetsch's terminology is double-edged: by

'deconstruction' he means not only a thematic dis-assembling of precon-
ceived regional stereotypes, but also the deconstruction of sedimented
linguistic and aesthetic icons. Kroetsch speaks of this reconsideration of
prairie poetics and identity as a process of 'un-naming,' and of
'demythologizing the systems that threaten to define people' ('Unhiding
the Hidden' 43). While insisting that existing language and systems of
representation be dismantled, Kroetsch is deliberately evasive in describing possible alternatives. He suggests that the prairie reality he is seeking
resists the inelasticity of any prescribed system because it is not a fixed
entity, but a process, a perpetual *becoming*: 'The whole business, I guess,
is one of capturing process,' he observes, and 'especially in a country like
Canada where things are being shaped but aren't already shaped, that's
very important' (Brown 7).

While Kroetsch only hints at a distinctive prairie poetics in his critical
writing, he demonstrates that poetics in his fiction. In addition to a
volume of poems entitled 'Seed Catalogue,' in which he aims to demonstrate poetically that on the Canadian prairie 'there are certain kinds of
things we can grow and certain things we can't grow' (MacKinnon 5), he
has written a series of three novels (which he refers to as a triptych rather
than a trilogy) devoted to portraying the Canadian prairie. Of these three
novels, *Gone Indian* most explicitly demonstrates Kroetsch's brand of
deconstruction. The title comes from a common phrase meaning to
renounce one's cultural heritage, and in the novel not only does Kroetsch
describe a character who 'goes Indian,' but he himself relinquishes
inherited conventions of representational fiction in order to give voice to
the prairie silence and shape to the prairie emptiness.

There is a deliberate irony in the title of his novel. 'Going Indian' for
Kroetsch entails not the abandonment of one culture in order to adopt
another, but a paradoxical interpenetration of cultures. On a thematic
level, *Gone Indian* describes a modern-day re-enactment of the Grey Owl
legend, according to which the Englishman Archie Belaney renounced
European cultivation to 'go Indian.' In *Gone Indian* a modern-day graduate student moves from Binghamton, New York, to Edmonton, where he
relinquishes his past in order to immerse himself in the local culture. But
Gone Indian retells the legend with a difference: Jeremy Sadness does not
willingly renounce one culture in favour of another, but finds himself
engulfed in a bewildering labyrinth of cultural multiplicity. Without
defying traditional realist strictures outright, Kroetsch deliberately juxtaposes and compounds levels of fictionality to the extent that the novel
parodies any attempt to fix prairie identity in a stable world conforming

to our expectations of representational fiction. Paradoxically, this insta-bility is attributed to the unique features that give the Canadian prairie an identity of its own.

Nothing in *Gone Indian* overtly contradicts the linear causality of tradi-tional novelistic plot. Jeremy is a graduate student whose thesis – consist-ing of the single unfinished sentence, 'Christopher Columbus, not knowing that he had not come to the Indies, named the inhabitants of that new world –' (21) – is being supervised by Professor Madham. Jeremy travels to Edmonton for a job interview, and once there he is distracted by a winter festival and adulterous affairs with both Jill Sunderman and her mother, Bea. After taking part in various incidents connected to the festival, Jeremy and Bea disappear on a snowmobile, never to be heard from again. While a confusion of identities and a proliferation of unlikely coincidences introduce considerable complexity to this representation of modern-day northern Alberta, at no point does Kroetsch overtly contra-dict novelistic conventions of verisimilitude. Instead, he exaggerates coincidence and juxtaposes such 'incommensurate orders of being' (McHale 80) as reality, dreams, and narrated fictions to the extent that the ground of the novel's fictional world is not the hard prairie earth we might expect, but a shifting matrix of dreams, myths, and cultural stereo-types.

A common postmodern technique is to assign multiple roles to a single character, thereby subverting traditional notions of a stable individual identity. In *The Sot-Weed Factor*, for example, John Barth offers a revisionist version of Maryland history by suggesting that such historical figures as Lord Baltimore, Henry Coode, and the Indian chief Powhatten were all in fact Henry Burlingame, a freelance entrepreneur who unwittingly became embroiled in political intrigue. In *Gone Indian* Kroetsch employs a variation of this postmodern technique: rather than assign multiple roles to a single character, he presents single roles that are apparently shared by multiple characters.

Jeremy arrives in Edmonton to find that he is carrying a suitcase belonging to Roger Dorck, a local lawyer. While the suitcase's real owner lies in a hospital bed, Jeremy takes Dorck's place as king of the winter festival and sleeps with both of Dorck's lovers. Jill Sunderman bears an uncanny resemblance to Carol, Jeremy's wife, and Professor Madham seems to have a double in Robert Sunderman: both men played hockey on the prairie as boys and dreamed of moving East (131). The stability of the characters' identities is further undermined by a collection of coincidences shared by multiple characters: a cowboy ski jumper, Roger

Dorck, and Jeremy all fall from a great height and land in the snow (Dorck and the ski jumper are in a coma); and at the end of the novel, both Jeremy and Robert Sunderman have disappeared, apparently having fallen through a hole in the ice. All of these characters inhabit an uncanny in-between state: Dorck hovers between life and death, other characters seem to be perpetually falling through the air, and Jeremy remains suspended in mid-sentence while he tries to complete his dissertation.

A more pervasive undermining instability in the novel's represented world involves not characters, but places. While the novel posits a verisimilar world in which Jeremy travels from Binghamton to Edmonton, at times the borders between East and West and between North and South appear to be permeable. In the novel's opening scene, for example, Madham and Carol visit the Binghamton zoo, where they observe a pair of buffalo. The roles of observer and observed are reversed when, as the buffalo look on, Madham and Carol 'romp on all fours' and play out a buffalo mating ritual on the grassy field before the buffalo enclosure. As Madham and Carol cavort, their surroundings resemble the Western prairie: Madham tosses Carol's clothes aside, 'as if with great bruising horns,' the sound of traffic recedes until it reminds the narrator of 'the rolling of thunder,' and the ground on which Madham and Carol romp is described as a grassy plain (2–3). Not only does the reversal of roles between buffalo and humans suggest the transgression of borders separating inside from outside (the caged buffalo become external observers while humans become an exhibit), but the apparent presence of the West in the East suggests the dissolution of geographic borders.

The novel's fictional world contains a complex layering of ontological levels, including dreams and various represented realities in the form of narrative fiction, myth, and the plastic arts, and the borders separating these various levels of reality within the novel's fictional world are tenuous. When Jeremy confronts an ice sculpture, an unexplained reference to the 'twinned hearts' of Jeremy and a sculpted buffalo suggests the transgression of conventional ontological borders: 'An Indian on a galloping horse bore down on a huge and galloping buffalo, leaned over both the buffalo and Jeremy, aimed an arrow of ice at their twinned hearts' (18). The Indian-and-buffalo scene recurs in a later passage, but this time as a dream. In his dream Jeremy finds himself once again beneath the poised spear of an Indian warrior, but in the dream Jeremy and the warrior are no longer separated by the ontological borders that distinguished the living Jeremy from the ice sculpture in the earlier scene: 'Poundmaker raised his feathered spear over the head of his sweating horse. Jeremy saw the flies swing lazily in the air, around the bloodied head of the spear' (109). The scene of Jeremy standing before a statue in the novel's represented 'real' world has migrated to a represented dream world, and in this dream world the exchange of identities hinted at with reference to the 'twinned hearts' becomes explicit: 'I was a *buffalo,*' Jeremy declares when recounting the dream to Madham (106).

Jeremy's dream not only implies the breach of a border separating dream from reality, but suggests an ontological transmigration on yet another level: Jeremy's dream is in fact the dramatization of a Blackfoot legend. The dream is attributed to the influence of a Blackfoot woman who sits silently beside Jeremy while he sleeps: 'He dreamed her dream' (101), the narrator explains. Ontological multiplicity is compounded when the Indian legend played out in Jeremy's dream turns out to be a re-enactment of the Binghamton zoo scene. In his dream Jeremy becomes the buffalo of legend and his mating with the Buffalo Woman bears an uncanny resemblance to the description of Madham and Carol at the zoo: 'He swung his horns into the matted sod. He pawed and gouged at the prairie with his hoofs and tossed up into the air the grass and the rooted clods' (107).

Kroetsch brings the ontological uncertainty of his fictional world one step closer to the real world of the novel's readers by deliberately blurring the identity of the novel's narrator through a complex structure of embedded narratives. The narrative framework is outlined in the novel's opening chapter: Madham addresses a letter to Jill Sunderman, in which he explains that the narration that follows is transcribed directly from audio tapes that Jeremy sent to Madham from Alberta. The narrative voice then alternates throughout the novel between Madham's first-person narration addressed to Jill Sunderman, and Jeremy's first-person narration addressed to Madham. The transition from one first-person narrator to the other is not always clearly indicated, and the effect is the blurring of borders separating narrator from narrated. For example, chapter 5 ends with Madham explaining, 'I sent him out there as on a mission, as on a veritable quest for something forever lost to me and yet recoverable,' and chapter 6 begins in the first person, with no grammatical or stylistic indication of a change of speaker: 'When I stepped from the air terminal' (14). The change of speaker can be logically deduced by the reference to the air terminal at which Jeremy lands in Alberta, but the repetition of the first-person pronoun causes at least momentary confusion of narrative levels.

The ambiguity of narrative levels comes even closer to the real world beyond the novel's pages with repeated hints of the presence of the author himself within the narrative. The fictional Professor Madham bears a striking resemblance to Kroetsch: both were raised in Alberta, were educated at the University of Alberta, and taught at Binghamton. The similarities go beyond autobiographic details to include narrative roles: both 'send' Jeremy back to Alberta 'as on a veritable quest for something forever lost to me and yet recoverable to the world' (14). Madham literally (within the novel's represented world) sends Jeremy back to the world of Madham's own boyhood, and Kroetsch figuratively 'sends' the character into a fictional world to retrieve the author's own past.

Jeremy's journey is not only portrayed as a personal quest to 'retrieve' the author's and/or the narrator's past, but is also compared to the historical quest for a New World, a quest originally undertaken by Columbus, and repeated more recently by Archie Belaney (a.k.a. Grey Owl). We are told repeatedly that Jeremy emulates the Englishman who renounced European civilization to 'go Indian,' and explicit parallels between Jeremy and Belaney are drawn when Jeremy trades his clothes for moccasins and a buckskin jacket and when he experiences a symbolic rebirth while shedding his clothes during a cross-country snowshoe race. The allegorical references reach further back in history with the reference to Columbus in the unfinished opening sentence of Jeremy's thesis. The implication is that like Grey Owl, and Columbus before him, Jeremy heads West in search of a New World.

Kroetsch's allegory, however, involves a revision of New World mythology. Just as Columbus had stumbled upon a world other than the one he was seeking, so Jeremy's latter-day quest takes him to a world that defies all his preconceptions. The represented world in which Jeremy's adventure transpires resembles the external world with which readers are familiar, but the apparent ambiguities of character and place, the permeable borders between sculpture, dream, and myth, and the ambiguities of narrative level all indicate an ontological instability undermining the notion of a secure world governed by predictable laws that is perpetuated by more traditional methods of realist representation.

Gone Indian's multiple, interpenetrating worlds are defined not only by geographic, but also by cultural borders: the novel's unsettling ontology results not so much from the blurring of borders between East and West as from the crossing of borders separating European from indigenous North American cultures. The zoo scene, for instance, suggests an unstable world not because of the displacement of the buffalo from the western plains to an eastern zoo (which can be accounted for in realistic terms), but because of the unaccounted-for migration of the buffalo from Indian legend to Jeremy's dream. Indian legend defines a world in which the Alberta prairie is populated by roaming herds of buffalo, and this world intrudes into the modern-day world of high-rise apartments and academic institutions through Jeremy's dream, Madham's imagination, the ice sculpture, and numerous rituals associated with the winter festival.

The de-centred world of *Gone Indian* is portrayed as the product of human responses to the prairie environment. When Madham observes that 'to get into a corner on those vast prairies is not easy' (95), he is speaking metaphorically, referring to the 'corner' Jeremy has backed himself into by lying about the completion of his thesis, by cheating on his wife, and by taking Dorck's place in local events that he knows nothing about. But the observation can be taken in a literal sense as well, as referring to the reaction of the settlers described by Harrison in *Unnamed Country* and by Ross in *As for Me and My House* to the prairie: the construction of artificial defences against the prairie nothingness. The predominant reaction to the prairie environment that *Gone Indian* describes is the need to find or build a vertical structure that breaks the horizontal monotony of the prairie horizon. Dorck's snowmobile accident is described as an escape from the horizontal plane of prairie life: 'Dorck turned towards a hummock of ice and snow. And he leaped up and over; like a dream of himself he climbed, into the night air, free of the earth at last' (26). Jeremy's snowmobile accident is described in strikingly similar detail: 'And then I was flying. All by myself I was sitting up there in the air, floating free. It seemed to last for a long time, that flight' (40). Yet another character takes to the air, this time a cowboy ski-jumper: 'And then he was up in the air, leaning forward, stiffly forward, so that his cowboy hat was over the tips of his skis. He kept on going up, up, then forward, then forward. The watching crowd gave out a gasp of wonder: that wild cowboy was riding nothing but the cold air, The arc of his rising, it seemed, would never break' (76).

In each of these descriptions, flying or falling involves a state of suspension: 'like a dream of himself he climbed ... free of the earth at last'; 'floating free. It seemed to last for a long time'; 'The arc of his rising, it seemed, would never break'. Similar states of suspension are described elsewhere in *Gone Indian* and are attributed to freezing. After crashing his snowmobile into a snowbank, Jeremy 'was rigid with cold. My arms were fixed at my sides, my legs were fixed, rooted in the loose snow ... I was inside a snowman, looking out on a strange, distant world' (40). These examples of suspended motion are similar to passages in Faulkner, except that in *Gone Indian* they are not attributed to idiosyncrasies of individual perception. These characters float, fly, and freeze not in their imaginations, but in actual events, events that are grounded in regional specificity: a buffalo jump, a ski jump, a snowmobile accident. And all are tied to the inherent need of the region's inhabitants to break free of the horizontal monotony of the prairie landscape.

These region-specific states of suspension are related to a nebulous moment, the instant between life and death, and this moment is associated with the act of narration. As he lies freezing in the snowbank, Jeremy compares his sensations to those of Scott, the Arctic explorer: 'Scott of the Antarctic, I thought to myself, inside your frail web of veins and arteries, the center of warmth grows smaller' (40). Through this freezing sensation Jeremy imagines Scott's last moments, in which the explorer relinquished narration in the face of death: 'You are right to make the last entry and close the notebook, let the pencil slip from your hand. You have only to listen now. Say no more. Listen to the fall of silence, hear your own last breath and know for one instant you are no longer' (40). But Jeremy does not relinquish narration; he prolongs that instant, and it is in such in-between moments that much of *Gone Indian* takes place.

These suspended states are prolonged throughout *Gone Indian*: just as Jeremy's thesis hangs suspended in mid-sentence, characters, by flying, falling, or freezing, hover between life and death. This suspended state corresponds to the 'impossible, purely *novelistic* instant' that Barthes describes, and Kroetsch ties that in-between state to regional specificity through references to geography (Edmonton as a border between East and West, and between North and South) and through climate (the numerous references to freezing). He also links the novel's represented world to the region with references to the region's distinct position in the cultural history of North America. Jeremy explains that 'two great waves of culture ... washed out from Europe, one to the east, one to the west. On the Great Central Plains of America they had met again' (103). It is at this meeting point of cultures that *Gone Indian* is situated. Its world is defined not by one or the other, but by the contradictory presence of both.

The world that Jeremy encounters when he arrives in Edmonton does not conform to a world defined by traditional New World mythology.

Neither an edenic world of new beginnings, nor a barbaric world awaiting civilization, the world of *Gone Indian* is not a 'new' world at all, but an 'other' world, a ground upon which multiple 'worlds' meet and interpenetrate. By linking that heterogeneous ontology to specific prairie characteristics, Kroetsch links a typically postmodern de-centred ontology to specificity of place. All of the traditional ingredients of regionalism – climate, geography, topography, history, and culture – come into play in Kroetsch's dis-covering of a distinct prairie ontology. *Gone Indian* is dedicated to depicting what one character refers to as 'the consequence of the northern prairies to human definition: the diffusion of personality into a complex of possibilities rather than a concluded self' (152). In the process of portraying a distinct being tied to a specific place, *Gone Indian* provides an alternative to the New World myths that have prevailed since Alencar and Cooper first used New World regions to dramatize conflicts between the New World and the Old.

LA REGIÓN MÁS TRANSPARENTE

Carlos Fuentes employs a de-centered ontology similar to Kroetsch's in order to depict a very different interpenetration of worlds in his novel *La región más transparente*. The central plateau of Mexico is the country's most distinctive geographic region. A naturally-formed truncated pyramid, the region provided the Aztecs with what they saw as the natural site for the centre of their empire. In the southwest corner of the plateau is a valley dotted with lakes, a region that the Aztecs referred to as 'Anáhuac,' from the Nahuatl word meaning 'near the water.' It was in this region that the Aztecs built Tenochtitlán, a centre of commerce and the home of Moctezuma, leader of an empire that spanned most of central Mexico when in 1519 Hernán Cortés and his army landed at Vera Cruz. After the last Aztec warrior had fallen in what is today Mexico City, Cortés found the central region suitable to house the powers that would rule New Spain. Today, Mexico City sits atop the ruins of Tenochtitlán. The site's layered history is graphically evident in the recently unearthed pyramid that juts through the city's central plaza.

At an elevation of nearly eight thousand feet and ringed by mountains, the site of Mexico's capital was not chosen for the convenience of commerce and industry, nor are its tropical climate and rocky, barren soil suited to agriculture. Yet since long before the conquest an overwhelming majority of the country's population has congregated in this central region, and inhabitants have accommodated themselves to the distinctive characteristics of geography, climate, and topography. These inhabitants not only have succeeded in wresting a subsistence from the inhospitable environment, but have built what is today one of the world's largest urban centres. An investigation of how the effects of the region's distinctive characteristics remain evident in today's Mexico City figures prominently in Fuentes's *La muerte de Artémio Cruz*; it also provides the central subject matter of his *Cambio de piel* and, most notably, *La región más transparente*. In this, his first novel, Fuentes juxtaposes the two worlds of Mexico City: the pre-conquest world of Aztec civilization and the present-day world of Mexico City.

The title of Fuentes's novel clearly defines its subject as the central plateau region of Mexico, and the phrase 'la región más transparente' has a rich history. It was popularized in the early twentieth century by Alfonso Reyes in his essay entitled 'El paisaje en la poesía mexicana del siglo XIX' ('Landscape in Nineteenth-Century Mexican Poetry'). Referring to the ancient Greek habit of inscribing welcoming messages over doorways, Reyes suggests that Mexico City's inhabitants might inscribe over their thresholds, 'Caminante, has llegado a la región más transparente del aire' (literally, 'Traveller, you have arrived at the region of the clearest air' [199]). Reyes's use of the phrase can be traced back to the eighteenth-century explorer Alexander von Humboldt (known in Mexico as Alejandro de Humboldt), who in turn may have borrowed it from an eighteenth-century poem by Manuel Navarette.[5] In choosing this phrase as the title of his novel, Fuentes not only designates the region as the subject of his narrative, but places his work in a tradition of fiercely nationalist literature: Reyes was a renowned nationalist essayist; the implicit reference to Humboldt acknowledges Mexico's colonial heritage; and Navarette's poem traces Mexican identity to Nahuatl culture, from which the Aztecs descended.

Inasmuch as its plot can be paraphrased, *La región más transparente* takes up the popular twentieth-century Mexican theme of '*la revolución traicionada*' (the betrayed revolution), placing the novel in a tradition of literature depicting the corruption of post-revolutionary Mexican society. *La región más transparente* describes a select group of corrupt Mexico City bureaucrats, as well as a few of the city's dispossessed, including a prostitute and a writer. The story of this group's exploits, however, does not account for the entire content of the novel. Furthermore, the story of Bobó, Rodrigo, the de Obandos, and their companions lacks the traditional narrative unity of conflict, climax, and denouement, and the narration is interrupted by disjointed shifts of narrative voice and focalization. A common view among critics is that the novel's narrative discontinuity is a deliberate reflection of the discontinuities in contemporary Mexican society, and that this technique allies *La región más transparente* with the many twentieth-century depictions of the fractious influence of ascendant industrialism and capitalism. Typical references to the mimetic function of *La región más transparente*'s narrative discontinuities include the following:

This structure is the reflection of a society in a state of decomposition, fragmentary, without any principles of a stable life. (C.S. Reyes 172)

The complicated structure ... offers us the social environment of Mexico City from 1951–'54 in all its reality ... This plurality of lives, of individual destinies corresponds to the plurality of times and places. (Luis Andrés Murillo, cited in C.S. Reyes 172–3)

To reflect the chaotic, violent, and absurd (in the eyes of Fuentes) life of the capital, the tale is interrupted, fragmented, converted into a giant puzzle of a thousand disparate pieces, juxtaposed, without apparent logic or chronological order. (Fell 371)

While such comments at least credit Fuentes with intentional disorder, they carry with them an implicit criticism of *La región más transparente*'s narrative structure as being fragmentary or incomplete. Samuel O'Neill voices this criticism explicitly when he faults one of the novel's central characters for a lack of verisimilitude: 'As a character, [Ixca] is not developed well psychologically' (cited by Sommers 289). Joseph Sommers cites O'Neill to back up his claim that the novel's entire narrative structure is wanting, and he concludes that 'Ixca Cienfuegos, the key character on whom the structure depends, lacks precision' (288).

Some critics have sought to find a unity underlying the novel's apparent disorder by considering the work not as the realistic representation of a present-day metropolis, but as the depiction of a mythological reality. Allusions to Mexico's Aztec heritage are obvious not only in the intertextual references of the novel's title, but also in the chapter titles, in characters' names, and even in references to Aztec rites, including human sacrifice. Fuentes is an avid student of Aztec mythology, and considerable research has been devoted to identifying correspondences between *La región más transparente* and Aztec mythology. In one of the most thorough examinations of the novel's mythological allusions, María Salgado explicates the entire novel as an updated narration of an Aztec myth. Salgado identifies one of the characters as a representation of the snake goddess and another character as her accomplice, and summarizes the novel's plot as the story of Teódula sending Ixca out to secure a human sacrifice. This mythological explication accounts for much of the novel's narrative complexity by identifying an undeniable subtext in *La región más transparente*, but it also suggests other weaknesses in the novel. If the novel's mythological dimension produces discontinuities that are discomforting to realists, to mythologists the novel's realistic dimension is entirely superfluous and detracts from the novel's deeper mythological significance. Salgado, for example, faults the novel's sketchy realism when she explains that 'the roles of Teódula and Ixca are consistent with the incorporation of myth into contemporary life,' but that 'Fuentes fails in trying to establish verisimilar relations between [Teódula and Ixca] and the rest of the characters' (235).

Both explications – the realistic and the mythological – fail to account adequately for the novel's narrative complexity. An alternative to both theories would be to seek a middle ground, to consider the novel not as a unidimensional representation of either a contemporary city or a mythological reality, but as a typically postmodern depiction of ontological multiplicity. Fuentes depicts a world of intersecting realities, and the region of the novel's title is uniquely suited to serve as the ground for that depiction. Just as Kroetsch portrays the Canadian prairie as a cultural, geographic, and ontological border land, Fuentes exploits Mexico City's unique geographic and historical situation in order to depict an in-between world. Mexico City is built atop traces of a previous civilization and on the surface *La región más transparente* is a realistic narrative, yet just beneath the novel's verisimilar narrative lies a complex mythological reality. This dual ontology is reflected not only thematically, in overt allusions to both Aztec mythology and '*la revolución traicionada*,' but also in the novel's language and narrative syntax. On the level of meaning, the specificity of place alluded to in the novel's title imparts a particular significance to this typically postmodern de-centred ontology.

A quick overview of the organization of *La región más transparente* explains why many critics feel justified in describing the novel as chaotic or fragmentary. Under three chapter headings, there are thirty-eight titled subchapters, and these in turn are divided into 104 textual segments set off by spaces within the text.[6] These various textual divisions contain a bewildering array of thoughts, voices, and transcribed texts. Despite this apparent narrative fragmentation, a close look reveals that meticulous care has been taken to provide continuity not only between segments, but also within larger textual divisions. Chronological order is broken up by many flashbacks and asides in the form of personal reminiscences, introspection, writings, and even one dream sequence, but even though these interruptions test the borders of traditional verisimilitude, they do not deny realistic representation outright. In the 'Federico Robles' subchapter of chapter 1, for example, there is a first-person, present-tense narration of a battle in the Mexican revolution; this, however, does not represent an unaccounted-for jump of some forty years in narrated time. In the paragraph immediately preceding the 'Federico Robles' subchapter, Ixca is on his way to visit Robles: 'Cienfuegos smiled and went into the pink stone building which soared high on Avenida Juárez between two old nineteenth-century homes' (71). The narrative present has already been established as 1951 ('ahora en el cincuenta y uno' [38]), and the location is unambiguously Mexico City. The 'Federico Robles' subchapter begins with Robles addressing his visitor: 'You ask me to go back to a very different time and place, Cienfuegos,' and this introductory paragraph ends with Robles saying, 'I hardly remember that I began there' (71). The lack of end punctuation and of a capital letter distinguishing this sentence from what follows may be disconcerting, but the shift from third-person narration to the first-person narration of the battle of Celaya is hinted at by Robles's spoken reference to his own memory, and is clearly indicated by the shift from roman to italic script. The twenty-five pages that follow contain some ambiguities with regard to focalization and voice – and I will return to these topics later – but despite shifts from a third-person account of the office and the spoken dialogue between Robles and Ixca to direct access to Robles's memory, the spatio-temporal orientation of the subchapter is unambiguous.

Narrative passages that deviate from a third-person account of present-day Mexico are consistently situated with reference to a narrative present. For example, the passage beginning 'They're dwarfs with long oily hair who hug us and dance on our bellies; the turkey talks to us from his amethyst throne' (161) – explicable only as deliberate obfuscation if considered in isolation – can be easily situated within the narrative framework of contemporary Mexico City. This passage occurs in the description of Gladys and Beto at Gladys's rented room; set off by italics, it comes after a reference to shared dreams ('We dream together,' [161]), and is immediately preceded by a description of both characters closing their eyes. Though to some this passage might represent an inexplicable jump from the streets of Mexico to a surreal world of pre-

Hispanic mythology, it is attributed to a dream shared by Gladys and Beto: a dream unambiguously situated in a room in contemporary Mexico City.

Similarly, an eight-page contemplation of the identity of Mexico is clearly attributed to Manuel; set in quotation marks, the passage begins on page 43 with '[Zamacoma] took up his pen,' and ends on page 49 with 'He folded his sheets of paper and stood.' And the dialogue around a café table on Paris Avenue, transcribed in movie-script format on pages 111–13 and page 117, is clearly linked to Rodrigo and his conversation with Ixca. This passage is once again set off in italics, and is introduced by, 'Rodrigo sniffed the rancid air and was carried back to those coffee tables on Paris [Avenue]' (111).

Rapid transitions between segments create the illusion of fragmentation in narrated space in *La región más transparente*, but a meticulous pattern of transitional links belies this perception. An overview of the 104 textual divisions reveals a pattern not immediately apparent in the novel's table of contents (which does not include the untitled segments): preceding almost every long segment is a shorter segment, sometimes identified by italicized titles, and sometimes untitled. These segments serve as transitional links, bridging what many perceive to be unexplained gaps between the textual segments.

The first such transitional segment appears on pages 8–9, between the subchapters entitled 'Gladys García' and 'El lugar del ombligo de la luna.' Beginning 'Out of the women's clothing store, onto the avenue'(8), this segment refers to Gladys's decision, described in the preceding paragraph, to look for a job as a sales clerk. It ends with a description of Norma and Pichi and the observation that 'they looked like gods who had risen like statues'(9), which projects ahead to the following subchapter, describing Norma and Pichi, among others, at Bobó's cocktail party.

The subchapter 'El lugar del ombligo de la luna' ends with the words, '"My father." My father, my father' (52); this introduces the next subchapter, the title of which ('Gervasio Pola') refers to Rodrigo's father. The repetition of 'My father ... my father ... my father'(62) at the end of the 'Gervasio Pola' subchapter brings the narrative back to Rodrigo and present-day Mexico. In the sentence that follows, the appearance of Pimpinela de Ovando on a nearby street ('Along Madero, Pimpinela de Ovando walked,' [62]) provides the transition to the next subchapter, 'Los de Ovando.'

The systematic linking of subchapters is more apparent in chapter 2, where the linking segments are identified in the table of contents; each of the first eleven subchapters is preceded by a shorter subchapter with an italicized title. The linking pattern continues through the novel, although the transitions sometimes take different forms. For example, the 'Feliciano Sánchez' subchapter is introduced by the closing words of the preceding subchapter, 'Para subir al nopal': 'Federico Robles was all alone ... inviolate in the last buttress of his consciousness, facing a memory which only today, the day of his downfall, could be summoned up' (301). When the next subchapter, 'Calavera de quince,' begins with the statement 'Dawn rose bright with sun, heavy with silence the morning after Robles, Zamacona, and Cienfuegos talked together in the café on Aquiles Serdán' (305), it is clear that the preceding 'Feliciano Sánchez' subchapter, an account of the execution of the man Robles condemned to death, was situated in the memory of Robles, either at the café while Manuel and Ixca continued to converse, or immediately thereafter.

Another perceived source of fragmentation in *La región más transparente* lies in its multiplicity of narrative voices. The novel's narration includes first-person interior monologue; apparently psychic, silent dialogue between characters; dreams; flashbacks; and apparently objective third-person narration. This variety of voices, however, might be attributed to a single source of narration: Ixca Cienfuegos. If Ixca does indeed fulfil the role of narrator, then he straddles both worlds: he is a participant in the represented reality of contemporary Mexico City, and he is omniscient owing to god-like qualities attributed to his role in Aztec mythology.

Ixca introduces himself unambiguously as the narrator in the novel's opening lines, 'My name is Ixca Cienfuegos' (3), and his role as observer in the novel would seem to support the conflation of his voice with that of the omniscient, third-person narrator of traditional realistic fiction.

Perhaps more than anything else, it is the open-ended plot of *La región más transparente* that invites criticism of the novel as unstructured. Flashbacks to the revolution and references to pre-Columbian civilization can be placed in the context of modern Mexico, but the story of Ixca, Robles, Rodrigo and the other characters has neither a beginning nor an end. Robles rises to power and falls; Rodrigo rises to wealth and fame; and Pimpinela regains her social standing by marrying wealth. There are dozens of such stories in *La región más transparente*, but none provides the novel with a central structure of conflict, climax, and denouement.

Traditional concepts of plot are based on the view of history as a linear progression, of each lifetime as having a beginning, a middle, and an end. The Aztec perception of time as cyclical, rather than linear, provides an alternative to these definitions of novelistic closure. Laurette Séjourné finds evidence of this cyclical temporality in what she refers to as 'the image of infinite cycles' that permeates Teotihuacan, the site of numerous temples just north of present-day Mexico City: 'these cycles, based upon the revolutions of the planets and upon laborious calculations, include the simplest – the yearly death and resurrection of Nature – and spread outward to embrace immense units' (92). The perception of a cyclical unity embracing all existence is graphically depicted in the Aztec calendar, as illustrated by the famous Piedra del Sol. This calendar comprises six circles: at the centre is an image of the fifth, or present sun; moving outward we find a second circle representing the four previous suns; a third circle contains the symbols for the days of the year; a fourth circle contains jade stones; a fifth circle depicts the sun's rays; and enclosing the entire calendar, a sixth circle is closed by a pair of inward-facing images of the fire serpent.[7]

La región más transparente displays a similar type of cyclical closure. We have already seen one example in the framing of the 'Gervasio Pola' subchapter between a repetition of the words 'My father' (52, 62). This is not an isolated example; it is just one frame within a vast system of frames. The narrative setting for the frame surrounding the 'Gervasio Pola' subchapter is Ixca and Rodrigo conversing, and the closure of the frame provides a transition when the focus subtly shifts to Pimpinela de Ovando walking along a nearby street. Comparing this transition on page 62 – 'Along Madero, Pimpinela de Ovando walked erect and perfumed, her eyes concealed behind tinted lenses, on her way to Roberto Regles's office' – to a similar passage on page 71 – 'Pimpinella, disguised by her dark glasses, just escaped meeting Ixca Cienfuegos' – it becomes apparent that the intervening section, the 'Los de Ovando' subchapter, is framed between two nearly identical scenes.

In the same way that the closure of the Rodrigo and Ixca frame provides a transition to Pimpinela and the 'Los de Ovando' subchapter, Pimpinela's chance encounter with Ixca leads into the next subchapter. Ixca passes Pimpinela on his way to Federico Robles's office, which provides the setting for the narration of the battle of Celaya from Robles's point of view. The pattern continues with Robles's mention of Norma at the close of the 'Federico Robles' subchapter: the narration shifts to Norma sunbathing, thus providing a transition to the 'Norma Larragoiti' subchapter, and the narrative returns on page 90 to Norma sunbathing, completing another frame. This succession of frames can be illustrated as shown in figure 1.

The closure of each of these frames is accompanied by a transition

Figure 1

52	┌─Rodrigo: 'My father.' My father, my father
52–62	│ 'Gervasio Pola'
62	│ Rodrigo: My father ... my father ... my
	└─ father ... →→→ Pimpinela walking

62	┌─Pimpinela walking
63–71	│ 'Los de Ovando'
71	└─Pimpinela walking →→→ Ixca and Robles

71	┌─Ixca and Robles
71–90	│ 'Federico Robles'
90	└─Ixca and Robles →→→ Norma sunbathing

90	┌─Norma sunbathing
90–6	│ 'Norma Larragoiti'
96	└─Norma sunbathing

propelling the reader's attention to the next narrative section. With the closing of the 'Norma sunbathing' frame, however, the forward progression is interrupted. This transitional segment not only returns our attention to a previous passage, and encloses the 'Norma Larragoiti' subchapter in a frame, but also refers back to page 42 and a third description of Norma sunbathing, thereby enclosing the 'Gervasio Pola,' 'Los de Ovando,' 'Federico Robles,' and 'Norma Larragoiti' subchapters, together with the intervening transitional passages, in a single frame. Adding this larger frame to figure 1, we can see an ever-expanding cyclical enclosure, as illustrated in figure 2.

The framing technique is pervasive throughout *La región más transparente*; as the novel moves from microstructure to macrostructure, it is possible to situate these internal frames within three larger frames. The first of these is comprised of the repetition of the words 'Here we bide. And what are we going to do about it. Where the air is clear' on pages 5 and 376, accompanied by a repeated description of Gladys García (stopping at a vendor's stall beside the Nonoalco Bridge to buy an aluminum cigarette holder on page 9, and then tossing a match from the bridge after lighting the night's last cigarette on pages 375–6).

The second frame is provided by Bobó's party. 'El lugar del ombligo de la luna' (10–49) describes a reunion of Mexico's elite at Bobó's in 1951, and beginning on page 350, the scene is repeated, this time in 1954

Figure 2

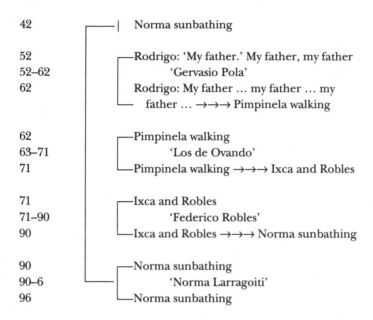

```
42                    ——|  Norma sunbathing

52                      ┌—Rodrigo: 'My father.' My father, my father
52–62                   │        'Gervasio Pola'
62                      │   Rodrigo: My father … my father … my
                        └—   father … →→→ Pimpinela walking

62                      ┌—Pimpinela walking
63–71                   │        'Los de Ovando'
71                      └—Pimpinela walking →→→ Ixca and Robles

71                      ┌—Ixca and Robles
71–90                   │        'Federico Robles'
90                      └—Ixca and Robles →→→ Norma sunbathing

90                      ┌—Norma sunbathing
90–6                    │        'Norma Larragoiti'
96                      └—Norma sunbathing
```

and with Jaime Ceballos and Betina Régules replacing Federico and
Norma as the rising stars of the high society.

And finally, within these frames is the Revolution of 1910. The narrative
returns to the Revolution primarily through the reminiscences of the
party's guests, and the biographical sketches of these guests advance
chronologically from the time of the Revolution to the present. Depicted
graphically the novel's macrostructure would look like this:

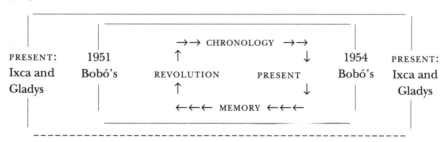

```
                              →→ CHRONOLOGY  →→
PRESENT:    1951          ↑                    ↓     1954    PRESENT:
Ixca and    Bobó's    REVOLUTION      PRESENT         Bobó's  Ixca and
Gladys                    ↑                    ↓              Gladys
                          ←←← MEMORY ←←←
```

While these frames impart a cyclical closure to the structure of the
novel, the key question of narrative voice remains unanswered. The
answer lies neither in mimesis nor in mythology, but in a combination of

the two. Ixca's words, 'Here we bide. What are we going to do about it. Where the air is clear,' provide a thematic unity to the novel; they define the subject of the novel as 'la región mas transparente del aire,' or Anáhuac, both of which designate the central plateau of Mexico where the capital city is located. The resignation to fate implicit in 'What are we going to do about it' – a statement, not a question – expresses the Aztec perception of time as a series of perpetually repeating cycles

A passage in 'El lugar del ombligo de la luna' gives an important clue to the identity of the novel's narrator. The passage is set apart by the use of italics, but unlike other such passages, there is no contextual link to a specific character. The passage reads as follows:

Through all their brains the same alcohol and the same forgetfulness flows, along with the same diluted blood; now beggars are horsed, and now all those so important little details of pins and handkerchief points, perfume and gesture and quotation, are all swirled together in the common pool of mutual jelly ... we know all excellent secrets and values, we're something, brother, something. We have every right to stomp on whomever we care to. (37–8)

This paragraph opens a new segment, and the paragraph that follows it offers a panoramic overview of the whole party, beginning with 'Jungle rhythm flooded the party' (38). A specific clue to the narrator's identity is provided by the reference to 'mutual jelly' (*la gelatina común*); it refers back to the novel's opening passage and to words directly attributed to Ixca, when he referred to the 'spirit of Anáhuac' (*duende de Anáhuac*) and a 'jelly of bones' (*gelatina de osamentas*).[8]

The single word 'gelatina' links the description of Bobó's guests to Ixca, and the cynical reference to a 'we' who have the right to 'stomp on whomever we care to' defines his critical attitude towards that which he narrates. This same attitude is apparent in third-person descriptions throughout the novel, particularly in descriptions of the streets of Mexico City such as 'The avenue was a cornucopia of refuse' (5), and 'The stink of vomit, sleep, heavy breathed air lifted the second the bus braked' (30).

Ixca's function in the novel is much like that of the matching fire serpents enclosing the Aztec calendar. The parallel is implicit in the name Cienfuegos, which alludes to Xiuhtecuhtli, or 'Señor Fuego,' god of fire (Fernández 61). Ixca presides over the cyclical structure of the novel the way Xiuhtecuhtli presided over the Aztec world; the mythologist Burr Cartwright Brundage explains that, as Lord of Time, Xiuhtecuhtli 'did not condemn men to inhabit an abstract time that marched endlessly on ... rather, he ... conveyed the sense of expressive intervals' (Brundage 25). The whole of Fuentes's novel can be seen not as fragmentary or incomplete, but as one of these time intervals, or cycles. Within this cycle, from the revolution to 1954, Robles rises to the height of his power, and then falls. This cycle is starting over again at the end of the novel when the next generation, represented by Jaime and Betina, takes up a position identical to that of Robles and Norma at the beginning of the novel. The cyclical rise and fall of Robles is described in the subchapters 'L'águila siendo animal' and 'El Aguila reptante,' which correspond to Aztec mythology's sun at its zenith and sun falling.

Ixca's role can be compared to the role of Tezcatlipoca, god of the smoking mirror in Nahuatl mythology. Like Tezcatlipoca, Ixca is omnipresent; he presides over confession, he is the controller of fate, and he is the image of humanity itself (Séjourné 168–9; Brundage 180). Throughout the novel there are allusions to a mysterious mist enshrouding the city:

She was not aware of the thin air or the steam floating from alleys and sewer covers nor the laden sky that nuzzled flat rooftops, nor the neons lighting a trembling night profile of a city that wanted to make her its own. (146)

A wisp of gas hissing from the inner patio past Rodrigo Pola's room, past the roof, up to the center of the sky, where it mixed with all the smells of the city. (62)

Like this mist permeating Mexico City, Ixca is everywhere; he envelopes the textual frames in an all-encompassing extra-textual frame, the ubiquitous 'spirit of Anáhuac.'

Over the past century, urban settings have frequently served to symbolize the corrupting influence of the ascendant powers of capital and industry. Zola's *Le Ventre de Paris* is the paradigm of this symbolic use of urban settings; Norris's *The Octopus* contains a similar use of urban imagery in its depiction of Hilda Hooven, who at the novel's conclusion wanders lost in San Francisco and – inevitably, it seems – turns to prostitution. Similar examples can be found in Federico Gamboa's *Santa,* set in Mexico, Dreiser's *Sister Carrie,* set in the United States, and countless other examples set in Europe and the Americas. There is certainly some of this use of urban imagery in *La región más transparente,* with its descriptions of garbage-lined streets and glimpses into the lives of the destitute. But the city in *La región más transparente* is more than a generic symbol;

specificity of place infuses the novel's urban environment with a particular meaning. Only in this city could these distinct realities collide and interpenetrate. In a dazzling depiction of the city's layered history, Ixca catches a glimpse of the two interpenetrating realities as he spins on his heels at the centre of the city's main plaza:

Palace, cathedral, Ayuntamiento building; the other disequal side of arched legs; half shadow forming an area of transient light, opaque, between the natural shadow of gray stone and worn marble. Across his eyes another scene hurried, violent, in flight; the flow of a dark canal to the south, filled with white tunics; on the north, a corner where stone broke into shapes of flaming shafts and red skulls and still butterflies: a wall of snakes beneath the twin roofs of rain and fire; to the west the castle of albinos and hunchbacks and peacocks and dried eagles' heads. Both images, both scenes, were strong in his eyes, and dissolved back and forth, each the mirror without background for the reappearance of the other. (196–7)

This powerful juxtaposition of alternate realities is grounded in real-world specificity of place. If one were to stand today in Mexico City's central plaza, one would be confronted by just such a collage of alternating images. *La región más transparente* portrays more than just these physical traces of Aztec society, though; the scene in the city's centre is only the surface evidence of an alternate world that permeates the entire world of the novel.

Fuentes portrays a heterogeneous ontology not only through descriptive passages like the one cited above, but also through language, narrative syntax, and narrative voice. The de-centred world of *La región más transparente* offers a revisionist history of Mexico by implying that, contrary to what is set forth in history books, the Spaniards did not conquer the Aztecs, that the conquest, colonization, the revolution, and 'la revolución traicionada' are merely one more cycle in a world ruled by indigenous gods.

CONCLUSION

It has been my aim to suggest that regionalism has exerted a significant influence on the development of New World literature. All of the examples I have examined fulfil traditional definitions of regionalism as works in which setting figures prominently, but these examples also dispel the unspoken assumption that an author preoccupied with the effect of a specific place on individual identity can produce only sentimental autobiography. These works indicate how regional specificity can shape New World fiction to reflect vital conflicts along borders that define personal, regional, and national identity.

New World regionalism began when romantic nationalists turned to local settings in their desire to express New World difference. In the novels of Alencar and Cooper, regional specificity added a distinctly New World flavour to the romantic quest for a transcendental union of man and nature. The primary goal of romantic regionalists was to 'civilize' the New World by integrating it into Western culture. National identity was a secondary consideration to romantic authors, and regional specificity was a mere afterthought.

Realist authors shifted the focus away from transcendent unity to concentrate more on regional specificity. Cunha and Norris employed regionalism to voice a subversive alternative to frontier mythologies, but their quest for difference was undone by the homogenizing perspective of their avowed 'disinterested' search for universal laws of existence. While the analytic gaze of empirical observation focused more specifically on local details, these details served a goal no less transcendent than that of romantic authors. Both Cunha and Norris approached their regions as storehouses of natural phenomena, and attempted to deny distinctions between book and world by naming these phenomena and filling the pages of their works with these names.

Modernists overturned realism's universalist assumptions and portrayed both self and region as autonomous enclaves of identity sheltered from an unknowable external world. Modernism's displacement of realism's external perspective brought to the fore the issue of regionalism's marginalization. From the early decades of the twentieth century through the 1940s and 1950s, New World regionalism increasingly became a literature of protest, aimed at the homogenizing forces of modernization housed in urban centres.

Postmodernism defines difference not as an autonomous refuge of identity, but as multiplicity. To the postmodernist author, a region is neither a symbol, nor an open book, nor a metaphor for the existential conflict between self and world. Instead it is the site of a loss of onto-logical monism, a source of heterogeneity. Postmodernists focus neither on book nor on world, but on the border that divides the two. Regionalism has inspired two prominent postmodern novelists in Robert Kroetsch and Carlos Fuentes, and examples of regionalism's influence can be found elsewhere in the Americas today. In the United States, John Barth owes much of his creative genius to his fascination with the geography and history of the Maryland coast; in Colombia, Gabriel García Márquez's literary career has been guided by a continued fascination with his native northern Colombia; and another example of regionalism's influence can be found in Jorge Amado's lifelong fascination with the social sub-strata of the Bahía region of northeast Brazil.

Today, an emerging interest in marginalized literatures is raising to prominence some of the issues that have been central to New World regionalism since its beginnings in the early nineteenth century. The works of Kroetsch and Fuentes provide just a hint of the influence that regionalism continues to exert on the development of a distinctive poetics of New World literature, and the works of these as well as other post-modern regionalists invite further investigation into the continued vitality of New World regionalism.

Notes

INTRODUCTION

1 In his famous 'Carta de Jamaica,' Bolívar describes the extraordinary circumstances of the descendants of the Spanish conquerors:

We are a small human species; we possess a world apart; surrounded by wide seas,
new in almost all the arts and sciences although in a manner old in the customs of
civil society ... We, who scarcely conserve vestiges of what we were in former times
and on the other hand, who are neither Indians nor Europeans but a middle species
between the legitimate owners of the country and the Spanish usurpers; in short,
being Americans by birth and our rights those of Europe, we have to dispute the
latter with those of the country and to maintain ourselves in it against the invasion of
the invaders; so we find ourselves in a most extraordinary and complicated position.
(39; this and all subsequent translations are my own, except where otherwise noted
in the bibliography.)

2 Ashcroft, Griffiths, and Tiffin outline three historical phases of postcolonial
literature: an 'imperial' period, marked by works produced by a literary
elite associated with the colonizing power; a later period marked by literature produced by 'natives' or 'outcasts' 'under imperial licence'; and a still
emerging stage that would abrogate the 'constraints of a discourse and the
institutional practice of a patronage system which limits and undercuts
their assertion of a different perspective' (6). The authors assert later that a
subversive element has always existed in postcolonial literature, but that
only recently has it become self-conscious: 'Ironically, it is only with the
fashion in Europe for subversive theory ... that post-colonial literatures have
begun ... to give credence to their own theories' (139).

3 The term commonly refers to the postcolonial author's position between cultures. Ashcroft et al. refer to 'a particular kind of "double vision" not available to uncolonized Indigenes. This vision is one in which identity is constituted by difference' (26). Slemon describes the emerging consensus among postcolonial theorists that 'the act of colonization, whatever its precise form, initiates a kind of double vision or "metaphysical clash" within the colonial culture, a binary opposition within language that has its roots in the process of either transporting a language to a new land or imposing a foreign language on an indigenous population' (12). Slemon attributes the phrase 'metaphysical clash' to Helen Tiffin (32).

4 See Hernán Cortés's letters and Bernal Díaz's personal account of the conquest of Mexico.

5 Although this group of Southern writers had an explicit regionalist political agenda which they hoped to further through literary means, even it is rarely referred to in American criticism as a regionalist movement. The only other North American association of writers that might be considered a concerted regionalist movement is a loosely knit collective of Canadian prairie writers and critics that published primarily in the 1970s, including Dick Harrison, Henry Kreisel, Robert Kroetsch, Robert Lecker, Eli Mandel, Roy Miki, and Laurence Ricou. Regionalism continues to flourish on the local level in every state and province, but these are the only two North American regionalist movements that have gained more than local prominence.

6 The three classic texts of avant-garde regionalism in South American literature are *La vorágine* (1924), by the Colombian José Eustacio Rivera; *Doña Barbara* (1926), by the Venezuelan Rómulo Gallegos, and *Don Segundo Sombra* (1929), by the Argentine Ricardo Guiraldes. For the definitive study of South American avant-garde regionalism in general, and these three texts in particular, see Alonso.

7 Slotkin develops this theory in *The Fatal Environment.*

8 Frye traces the historical origins of a 'garrison mentality' in his conclusion to *Literary History of Canada,* and describes the effects of this mentality on contemporary Canadian literature in his preface to *The Bush Garden.*

9 I made the difficult decision to exclude Quebec fiction from my study of New World regionalism only because space did not permit an adequate discussion of this rich body of fiction and criticism. The Québécois *roman de la terre* is the exception to my earlier observation that North America has no significant history of regionalist literature. See Söderlind for an excellent theoretical discussion that situates Quebec regionalism in the context of New World settlement.

10 See especially Schlenz's discussion of her *Starry Night.*

11 Philip Fisher, for example, alludes to the cultural 'space' inhabited by Hispanics, gays, and other marginalized segments of American culture in his discussion of 'the new regionalisms.' At a special session at the 1991 Modern Language Association meeting, a panellist spoke of the space described in Woolf's *A Room of One's Own* as a kind of regionalism.

12 The *Oxford English Dictionary* defines 'region' as 'A large tract of land ... a more or less defined part of the earth's surface, now esp. as distinguished by certain natural features, climatic conditions, a special fauna or flora, or the like ... An area, space or place, of more or less definite extent or character.' W.J. Keith voices a traditional definition of literary regionalism when he designates as regionalist 'novels or series of novels that succeed in creating an imaginative world which is unique in that it establishes its own "reality" ... but taking its origin from a recognizable stretch of countryside' (11).

13 For an authoritative survey of recent works on bioregionalism, see Kowalewski.

14 For a thorough survey and well reasoned critique of some of the most recent back-to-nature movements, see Martin Lewis's *Green Delusions.* His tabular appendix (pp. 253–6), contrasting 'Arcadian' or radical environmentalism to 'Promethean' or what he believes to be a more realistic environmentalism, provides a convenient, if exaggerated, summary of the more radical positions.

CHAPTER 1   A World Apart

1 René Wellek is one of many critics who trace the origins of romanticism to German thought; he explains that 'romanticism in Germany was far more pervasive than in the other countries,' and concludes that 'romanticism was more completely victorious in Germany than elsewhere for very obvious historical reasons' ('The Concept of "Romanticism"' 166–7).

2 Coleridge, for example, on the one hand describes allegory as merely pointing to superficial similarities, and declares that 'allegory is but a translation of abstract notions into a picture language ... the principal being more worthless even than its phantom proxy.' He describes the symbol, on the other hand, as being 'characterized by a translucence of the special in the individual ... above all by the translucence of the eternal through and in the temporal' (468).

3 Paul de Man challenges traditional wisdom by suggesting that the favoured trope among romantics was not the symbol, but allegory, which he defines as the deferral of presence through purely linguistic, or intertextual, reference (in 'The Rhetoric of Temporality').

4 The Portuguese *sertão* translates literally as 'backlands.' In Brazil the term
   has particular connotations: it designates a particular region in the Northeast known for its harsh climate and rugged topography. To preserve these
   specific connotations, I will use the Portuguese term throughout, together
   with the accompanying term *sertanejo*, which refers to the inhabitants of the
   region.
5 Cândido identifies Magalhães's critical writings as 'the starting point of a
   theory of literary nationalism' ('Formação' 13).
6 'Indigenism' is a well documented tradition in South American literature.
   It springs from the same quest for an autochthonous literature that led to
   regionalism. Although some North American novelists, such as James Fenimore Cooper, experimented with 'Indian' novels, the genre is not as established in North America as it is in South America.
7 Alencar was responding in particular to Franklin Távora, who referred to
   Alencar's 1870 novel, *O gaúcho*, as 'literatura do gabinete' ('closet literature') and who criticized Alencar for pretending to be an authority on a
   region he had only envisioned from within the comfort of his own study.
   Távora's criticism of *O gaúcho* appears in the second of eight letters published between September and October 1871 in a Rio de Janeiro journal,
   Questões do dia. The letters, signed with the pseudonym 'Semprônio,' were
   addressed to 'Cincinato,' a pseudonym for José Feliciano de Castilho, the
   journal's editor. See José Maurício Gomes de Almeida for a discussion of
   Távora's 'Cartas a Cincinato' (72).
8 José Maurício Gomes de Almeida observes that in both his indigenism and
   his regionalism Alencar's objective was always 'through glorifying a regional
   type, [to] construct a myth of national significance' (53). In *O sertanejo*,
   'Alencar's strategy for building his mythic *sertanejo* always relies on this
   technique of drawing a parallel either implicit or explicit – between situations or characters in the novel and situations and characters the author
   seeks in the mythic repertoire of European myth' (58).
9 In her discussion of Cooper, Annette Kolodny notes the sexual analogies
   and presents compelling evidence that throughout the novel Cooper is
   describing a figurative rape of the land. The question remains, however,
   whether Cooper is celebrating or condemning this rape (101–5).
10 Although the ironic use of notes to parody the narrator's supposed authority is a common fictional technique, there is no hint of such irony in *The
   Prairie*; the notes are consistent with the didactic intentions described in
   Cooper's lengthy historical introduction.
11 Citing plot improbabilities and inconsistencies in Cooper's dialogue has
   been a favourite pastime of critics. One of Cooper's earliest critics was

Mark Twain, who declared that 'Cooper's eye was splendidly inaccurate' (cited by John William Ward in his 'Afterword' to the Signet edition of *The Prairie* 405). Nevertheless, certain details do attest to some detailed knowledge of his subject: Cooper's careful distinction of over half a dozen different Indian bands, for example, is far from the 'noble savage' stereotype, and some of his descriptive details do ring true. Anyone who has seen a buffalo's darting eyes on the other side of a zoo enclosure, for example, will understand the terror of Dr Bat at seeing these 'horrible eyes' up close as a rampaging buffalo stampedes past him (211).

CHAPTER 2   Regions from Afar

1 See chapter 1, note 7.
2 Domingos José Gonçalves de Magalhães, *Niterói, Revista Brasiliense de Ciências, Letras e Artes*, 1836, quoted by Antônio Cândido in his *Formação da Literatura Brasileira*, Vol. II, p 13.
3 As Costa Lima's translator explains, the author uses the term 'mimesis' 'in a broad manner to deal with the poetics of literature, literary theory, and historiography within a wide chronological frame' (xv). Costa Lima's thesis is (very roughly) that inscribed practice among literary criticism dictates the perpetuation of tradition, and that this reproduction of inherited standards constitutes mimesis. A 'mimetizable agent' is thus an author whose works are susceptible of being absorbed into such a self-perpetuating tradition.
4 I refer in particular to a definition formulated by George Stewart: 'A closer definition of regionalism would require the work of art not only to be nominally located in the region but also to derive actual substance from that location' (370–1). See also the 'mystery of place' alluded to by William Everson, which will be discussed in more detail later in this chapter.
5 Referring to Zola's Rougon-Macquart series, James observed that 'fiction so conducted is in fact a capacious vessel. It can carry anything' (95).

CHAPTER 3   Inside Out

1 This was not necessarily a city/country rivalry: see Sarabia for an example of urban avant-garde regionalism in Buenos Aires.
2 The significance of this regionalist conference is the subject of some debate. The 'Manifesto Regionalista,' which Freyre claims as the singular accomplishment of the conference, was not published until several years afterward, and Freyre's critics suggest that he in fact fabricated the manifesto in order to raise what had merely been an impromptu gathering of

local artisans to the stature of a national conference. Whether or not Freyre consciously orchestrated a regionalist movement, there is no denying that his interest in Northeast regionalism had a decisive influence on the Northeast authors of the 1930s.

3 'The repercussion of the "modernism" of Rio and São Paulo was insignificant on this regional group' (*Região e tradição* 61).

4 The opening sentence of *O sertanejo* reads as follows: 'That immense plain, that extends toward unending horizons, is the sertão of my native land' (1019).

5 A typical description of the novel is that of Fred Ellison: '*Parched Lives* is made of disconnected scenes. Each chapter ... has its own unity, its own near-independence, and might be said to constitute a short story, in which action is less important than the study of the psychological make-up of the character' (131).

6 'The chapters must follow a very particular order because the structure of the novel adopts the cyclical form of drought and flood that is characteristic of the region treated in *Vidas sêcas*' (Williams, cited by José Maurício Gomes de Almeida 248).

7 Lins do Rêgo describes his first meeting with the famous sociologist as the beginning of his literary career: 'For me my literary existence had begun that evening of our encounter ... That life began to act on mine with such intensity, with such force, that without knowing it I watched my personality dissolve, thinking as he did, resolving everything, constructing everything as he did' (Lins do Rêgo's preface to Freyre's *Região e Tradição* 32).

8 Fred Ellison, for example, asserts that 'the fact that Vitorino reminds us of Cervantes' great man of La Mancha is sufficient proof of the inherent literary worth of the novel' (75).

9 According to 1990 census figures, 14,775,997 of the country's 81,883,000 inhabitants live in metropolitan Mexico City. *1991 Britannica Book of the Year* (Chicago: Encyclopaedia Britannica, 1991).

CHAPTER 4   The Poetics of Place

1 Frank first outlined his theory in 1945. For a bibliography of the debate between Frank and his critics that spanned three decades, see Smitten and Daghistany 248–63.

2 'It may be true of all long discourses that their significance is not determined by "linguistic sequence." It is determined by the interrelation of parts, certainly; but this is true whether it is said of *The Wasteland* or of *Middlemarch*. The fact that one of these works possesses extensive narrative

continuity and the other does not makes no difference to this point' (Kermode 582).

3 Examples include Kathleen Lenore Komar, 'The Multilinear Novel: A Structural Analysis of Novels by Dos Passos, Döblin, Faulkner, and Koeppen,' *DAI* 38 (1977); John Michael Lannon, 'William Faulkner: A Study in Spatial Form,' *DAI* 33 (1973); Frances Elam Neidhardt, 'Verbal-Visual Simultaneity in Faulkner's *The Sound and the Fury*: A Literary Montage Filmscript for Quentin,' *DAI* 39 (1978); and Jimmie E. Tanner, 'The Twentieth Century Impressionistic Novel: Conrad and Faulkner,' diss., University of Oklahoma, 1964.

4 See Kartiganer, Kinney, and Ruzicka.

5 Tick describes *Go Down, Moses* as 'a unified narrative,' but qualifies his observation by adding that 'this pertains to only six of the "sections"' (328). Having conveniently discarded 'Pantaloon in Black' from his unifying framework, Tick goes on to insist that no other chapter can be considered in isolation.

6 In Chapter 8 of 'Initiation and Identity: *Go Down, Moses* and *Intruders in the Dust*,' Vickery describes a thematic unity in that every chapter is based on the theme of the hunt. She refers to the novel as 'loosely constructed' on p. 124.

7 Kuyk refers to Faulkner's distinctive use of narrative voice in his discussion of *Go Down, Moses*'s multiple fabula. Michael Millgate offers an argument for unity in the novel based on point of view: by attributing apparent contradictions in the novel to diverse sources of information, Millgate describes unresolved tensions in the novel as the result of conflicting 'points of view.'

8 Watson discusses her intentions in 'What I'm Going to Do,' and in 'It's What You Say.'

9 In 'What I'm Going to Do,' Watson says that in *The Double Hook* she wanted to demonstrate 'how people are driven, how if they have no art, how if they have no tradition, how if they have no ritual, they are driven in one of two ways, either towards violence or towards insensibility' (15).

10 Grace refers to the novel's 'universal mythic quality,' and describes the novel's narrative as a 'movement from violent *Aufbruch* to apocalyptic destruction ... and then on to rebirth and renewal' (208).

11 Grace compares James's return at the novel's conclusion to the traditional theme of 'hero ever-returning to wife, child and home' (208), and describes the birth of Lenchen's child as a nativity scene (196).

CHAPTER 5   Multiple Worlds

1 Alan Wilde uses the term 'middle ground' to designate 'fiction that rejects

equally the oppositional extremes of realism on the one hand and a world-denying reflexivity on the other, and that invites us instead to perceive the moral, as well as the epistemological, perplexities of inhabiting and coming to terms with a world that is itself ontologically contingent and problematic' (4). The two poles of the dual opposition that Wilde identifies correspond roughly to Kroetsch's distinction between 'books that contain the idea of world' and those that contain 'the idea of book,' or the distinction I have been making between external and internal approaches to representing regions.

2 For Spanos the aim of modernist 'spatial form' is 'to raise the reader above the discontinuities of temporal life' (*Repetitions* 32).

3 Spanos explains the implications of postmodernism's engagement with historicity by tracing the etymology of the word 'interest' to its roots in the latin *inter esse*, or 'being in the midst.'

4 These two examples are from stories by Guy Davenport, 'The Haile Selassie Funeral Train' and 'The Invention of Photography in Toledo' (McHale 45, 47).

5 Talking about the proximity of Mexico City to the two Nevados de la Puebla Mountains, Humboldt describes the region's rarefied air: 'This proximity contributes greatly to the formidable and majestic appearance of the Mexican volcanoes. The contours of their peaks, perpetually covered in snow, are much more pronounced since the air, across which the light reaches our eyes, is thinner, more transparent' (247–8).

Fray Manuel de Navarrete, an eighteenth-century Mexican poet, in his poem 'La mañana,' describes 'una luz resplandeciente / que hace brillar la cara de los cielos' (roughly translated: 'a resplendent light / that shines from the visage of the heavens'; cited by Reyes in his 'Visión de Anáhuac' 99).

6 For the sake of consistency, I will retain the terms 'chapter,' 'subchapter,' and 'segment' throughout to distinguish these three categories of textual divisions.

7 Paraphrased from Fernández, 25.

8 My translation. Hileman has translated 'gelatina de osamentas' as 'jelly of your own courage.' My more literal translation acknowledges the reference to Aztec rituals.

Barthes, Roland. *The Pleasure of the Text.* Trans. Richard Miller. New York: Hill and Wang, 1975.

Bergson, Henri. *Essais sur les Données Immédiates de la Conscience.* 1889. Paris: Librairies Félix Alcan, 1909.

Bertens, Hans, and Douwe Fokkema, eds. *Approaching Postmodernism: Papers Presented at a Workshop on Postmodernism, 21–23 September, 1984, University of Utrecht.* Amsterdam: John Benjamins, 1986.

Bolívar, Simón. 'Carta de Jamaica.' *El pensamiento del libertador.* Ed. Ignacio de Guzmán Noguera. Vol. 1. Bogota: Biblioteca de Autores Colombianos, 1953. 103–4. 2 vols.

Bradbury, Malcolm. 'Modernisms/Postmodernisms.' *Innovation and Renovation: New Perspectives on the Humanities.* Ed. Ihab Hassan and Sally Hassan. Madison: U of Wisconsin P, 1983. 311–27.

Brooks, Cleanth. *William Faulkner: The Yoknapatawpha Country.* New Haven: Yale UP, 1963.

Brown, Russell M. 'An Interview with Robert Kroetsch.' *University of Windsor Review* 2 (1972): 1–8.

Brundage, Burr Cartwright. *The Fifth Sun: Aztec Gods, Aztec World.* Austin: U of Texas P, 1979.

Cândido, António. *Formação da Literatura Brasileira.* 2nd ed. São Paulo: Martins, 1964.

– 'Backwardness and Underdevelopment: Its Repercussions in the Writer's Consciousness.' *Latin America in Its Literature.* Ed. César Fernández and Julio Ortega. Trans. Mary G. Berg. New York: Holmes and Meier, 1980. 263–82.

Castello, José Aderaldo. Introduction. *Menino de Engenho.* By José Lins do Rêgo. 8th ed. Rio De Janeiro: José Olympio Editôra, 1965. xviii–c.

Coleridge, Samuel Taylor. 'The Statesman's Manual.' 1816. Rpt. in *Critical Theory since Plato.* Ed. Hazard Adams. New York: Harcourt, 1971. 467–71.

Cooper, James Fenimore. *The Prairie.* 1827. Toronto: Signet-NAL, 1964.

Cortés, Hernán. *Hernán Cortés: Letters from Mexico.* Trans. Anthony Pagden. New Haven: Yale UP, 1986.

Costa Lima, Luis. *Control of the Imaginary: Reason and Imagination in Modern Times.* Trans. Ronald W. Sousa. Theory and History of Literature 50. Minneapolis: U of Minnesota P, 1988.

Cunha, Euclides da. *Os sertões.* 1900. Rpt. as *Rebellion in the Backlands.* Trans. Samuel Putnam. Chicago: U of Chicago P, 1944.

Davidson, Donald. 'Regionalism and Nationalism in American Literature.' 1938. Rpt. in *Still Rebels, Still Yankees and Other Essays.* N.p.: Louisiana State UP, 1972. 267–78.

de Man, Paul. 'The Rhetoric of Temporality.' In his *Blindness and Insight: Essays*

Works Cited

Abrams, M.H. *The Mirror and the Lamp: Romantic Theory and the Critical Tradition.* London: Oxford UP, 1953.
- *A Glossary of Literary Terms.* New York: Holt, Rinehart, and Winston, 1957; 3rd ed., 1971.
Aiken, Conrad. 'William Faulkner: The Novel as Form.' *William Faulkner: Four Decades of Criticism.* Ed. Linda Welshimer Wagner. N.p.: Michigan State UP, 1973. 134–40.
Alencar, José de. *O guaraní.* 1857. Rpt. in *Obra Completa de José de Alencar.* Vol. 2. Rio de Janeiro: José Aguilar, 1960. 25–280. 4 vols. 1958–60.
- *Os filhos de Tupã.* 1863. Rpt. in *Obra.* Vol 1. 561–73.
- *Sonhos d'ouro.* 1872. Rpt. in *Obra.* Vol. 1. 689–940.
- *O sertanejo.* 1875. Rpt. in *Obra.* Vol. 3. 1011–260.
Almeida, José Américo de. *A bagaceira.* 1928. Rpt. as *Trash.* Trans. R.L. Scott-Buccleuch. London: Peter Owen, 1978.
Almeida, José Maurício Gomes de. *A Tradicão Regionalista no Romance Brasileiro.* Rio de Janeiro: Achiamé, 1981.
Alonso, Carlos J. *The Spanish American Regional Novel: Modernity and Autochthony.* New York: Cambridge UP, 1990.
Andrade, Mario de. *Macunaíma, o herói sem nenhum caráter.* 1928. São Paulo: Secretaria de Cultura, Ciência e Tecnologia, 1978.
- 'De antrofagía.' *Diário de São Paulo.* 12 June 1929: 4.
Ashcroft, Bill, Gareth Griffiths, and Helen Tiffin, eds. *The Empire Writes Back; Theory and Practice in Post-Colonial Literatures.* New York: Routledge, 1989.
Assis, Machado de. 'Noticia da Atual Literatura Brasileira: Instinto de nacion lidade.' 1873. Rpt. in *Obra Completa.* Rio de Janeiro: José Aquilar, 1962. 801-
Austin, Mary. 'Regionalism in American Fiction.' *English Journal* 21 (Feb. 193! 97–106.

in the Rhetoric of Contemporary Criticism. Minneapolis: U of Minnesota P, 1971. 187–228.

Díaz, Bernal. *The Conquest of New Spain.* Trans. J.M. Cohen. London: Penguin, 1987.

Ellison, Fred P. *Brazil's New Novel: Four Northeastern Masters.* Berkeley: U of California P, 1954.

Emerson, Ralph Waldo. *Nature.* 1836. Rpt. in *The Collected Works of Ralph Waldo Emerson.* Vol. 1. Cambridge, MA Belknap P of Harvard UP, 1971. 7–45. 3 vols.

Everson, William. 'Archetype West.' *Regional Perspectives: An Examination of America's Literary Heritage.* Ed. John Gordon Burke. Chicago: American Library Association, 1973. 49–75.

Faulkner, William. *Go Down, Moses.* 1942. New York: Vintage, 1973.

Fell, Claude. 'Mito y realidad en Carlos Fuentes.' *Homenaje a Carlos Fuentes: Variaciones interpretativas en torno a su obra.* Ed. Helmy F. Giacoman. New York: L.A. Publishing, 1971. 365–76.

Fernández, Adela. *Dioses prehispánicos de México: mitos y deidades del panteón nahuatl.* Mexico: Panorama Editorial, 1983.

Fisher, Philip. Introduction. *The New American Studies: Essays from Representations.* Ed. Philip Fisher. Berkeley: U of California P, 1991. vii–xxii.

Frank, Joseph. 'Spatial Form in Modern Literature.' 1945. Rpt. in *The Widening Gyre.* New Brunswick, NJ: Rutgers UP, 1968. 3–62.

– 'Spatial Form: An Answer to Critics.' *Critical Inquiry* 4 (1977): 231–52.

Freyre, Gilberto. *Manifesto Regionalista.* 1926. Recife: Instituto Joaquim Nabuco de Pesquisas Sociais, 1967.

– *Região e tradicão.* 1941. Rio de Janeiro: Gráfica Record Editora, 1968.

Frye, Northrop. *Literary History of Canada.* Ed. Carl F. Klinck. Toronto: U of Toronto P, 1965.

– *The Bush Garden.* Toronto: Anansi, 1971.

Fuentes, Carlos. *La región más transparente.* 1958. Rpt. as *Where the Air Is Clear.* Trans. Sam Hileman. New York: Farrar, 1964.

Gadamer, Hans-Georg. *Truth and Method.* Trans. and ed. Garrett Barden and John Cumming. New York: Seabury, 1975.

Garland, Hamlin. *Crumbling Idols: Twelve Essays on Art and Literature.* 1894. Gainesville, FL: Scholars' Facsimile & Reprints, 1957.

– *Main-traveled Roads.* 1891. New York: Harper, 1899.

– 'A New Declaration of Rights.' *The Arena* 3.14 (Jan., 1891): 157–84.

– 'Local Color as the Vital Element of American Fiction.' *Proceedings of the American Academy of Arts and Letters and the National Institute of Arts and Letters.* No. 4 (N.p.: n.p., 1910–11). 41–5.

Grace, Sherrill. 'Sheila Watson and the "Double Hook" of Expressive Abstraction.' *Regression and Apocalypse: Studies in North American Literary Expressionism.* Toronto: U of Toronto P, 1989. 185–209.

Grove, Frederick Philip. *Settlers of the Marsh.* Toronto: Ryerson, 1925.

– *Our Daily Bread.* Toronto: Macmillan, 1928.

– *It Needs to Be Said.* 1929. Ottawa: Tecumseh, 1982.

Harrison, Dick. *Unnamed Country: The Struggle for a Canadian Prairie Fiction.* Edmonton: U of Alberta P, 1977.

Heidegger, Martin. *Being and Time.* Trans. John Macquarrie and Edward Robinson. New York: Harper, 1962.

Hoffmann, Gerhard, Alfred Hornung, and Rüdiger Kunow. ' "Modern," "Postmodern," and "Contemporary" as Criteria for the Analysis of 20th Century Literature.' *Amerikastudien* 22 (1977): 19–46.

Howells, William Dean. 'Criticism and Fiction.' *Criticism And Fiction and Other Essays.* Ed. Clara Marburg Kirk and Rudolf Kirk. New York: New York UP, 1959. 9–87.

Humboldt, Alejandro de. *Ensayo Politico sobre el reino de la Nueva España.* Mexico: Editorial Pedro Robredo, 1941.

James, Henry. 'Emile Zola.' 1903. Rpt. in *Theory of Fiction: Henry James.* Ed. James E. Miller, Jr. Lincoln: U of Nebraska P, 1972.

Kaliman, Ricardo J. 'Unseen Systems: Avant-garde Indigenism in the Central Andes.' *Representing Regionalism: New Approaches to the Field.* Ed. David Jordan. New York: Garland, forthcoming.

Kartiganer, Donald M. *The Fragile Thread: The Meaning of Form in Faulkner's Novels.* Amherst: U of Masssachusetts P, 1979.

Keith, W. J. *Regions of the Imagination.* Toronto: U of Toronto P, 1988.

Kermode, Frank. 'A Reply to Joseph Frank.' *Critical Inquiry* 4 (1978): 579–88.

Kinney, Arthur F. *Faulkner's Narrative Poetics: Style as Vision.* Amherst, U of Massachusetts P, 1978.

Kolodny, Annette. *The Lay of the Land: Metaphors as Experience and History in American Life and Letters.* Chapel Hill: U of North Carolina P, 1975.

Komar, Kathleen Lenore. 'The Multilinear Novel: A Structural Analysis of Novels by Dos Passos, Döblin, Faulkner, and Koeppen.' *DAI* 38 (1977), 2101A.

Kowalewski, Michael. 'Bioregional Perspectives.' *Representing Regionalism: New Approaches to the Field.* Ed. David Jordan. New York: Garland, forthcoming.

Kroetsch, Robert. *Gone Indian.* Toronto: New P, 1973.

– 'Unhiding the Hidden: Recent Canadian Fiction.' *Journal of Canadian Fiction* 3 (1974): 43–5.

Kuyk, Dirk, Jr. *Threads Cable-Strong: William Faulkner's* Go Down, Moses. Lewisburg: Bucknell UP, 1983.

Lewis, Martin W. *Green Delusions: An Environmentalist Critique of Radical Environmentalism.* Durham: Duke UP, 1992.

Lins do Rêgo, José. *Fogo morto.* 1943. Rio de Janeiro: Liv. José Olympio Ed., 1973.

McHale, Brian. *Postmodernist Fiction.* New York and London: Methuen, 1987.

McHaney, Thomas L. 'Faulkner and Modernism: What Does It Matter?' *New Directions in Faulkner Studies: Faulkner and Yoknapatawpha, 1983.* Ed. Doreen Fowler and Ann J. Abadie. Jackson: UP of Mississippi, 1984. 37–60.

MacKinnon, Brian. ' "The Writer Has Got to Know Where He Lives": An Interview with Robert Kroetsch.' Pt. 1. *Writer's News Manitoba* 1 (1982): 3–18.

Mandel, Eli. 'The Regional Novel: Borderline Art.' In *Taking Stock.* Proc. of The Calgary Conference on the Canadian Novel. Feb. 1978. Ed. Charles R. Steele. Downsview, Ont.: ECW, 1982. 103–20.

Maxwell, D.E.S. 'Landscape and Theme.' *Commonwealth Literature: Unity and Diversity in a Common Culture.* Ed. John P. London: Heinemann, 1965. 82–9.

Miki, Roy. 'Prairie Poetics: An Interchange with Eli Mandel and Robert Kroetsch.' *Dandelion* 2 (1983): 82–92.

Millgate, Michael. *The Achievement of William Faulkner.* London: Constable and Co., 1960.

Mitchell, W.J.T. 'Spatial Form in Literature: Toward a General Theory.' *Critical Inquiry* 6 (1980): 271–99.

Mitchell, W.O. 'Regionalism and the Writer: A Talk with W.O. Mitchell.' *Canadian Literature* 14 (1962): 51–63.

Norris, Frank. *The Octopus: A Story of California.* 1901. New York: Penguin Books, 1986.

– 'An Opening for Novelists: Great Opportunities for Fiction Writers in San Francisco.' 1897. Rpt. in *Novels and Essays: Frank Norris.* Ed. Donald Pizer. New York: Library of America, 1986. 1112–14.

O'Neill, Samuel. 'Psychological-Literary Techniques in Representative Contemporary Novels of México.' Diss. U of Maryland, 1965.

Paz, Octavio. *El laberinto de la soledad.* Mexico: Fondo de Cultura Económica, 1959.

Ramos, Graciliano. *Vidas sêcas.* 1938. Rpt. as *Barren Lives.* Trans. Ralph Edward Dimmick. Austin: U of Texas P, 1965.

Ransom, John Crowe. 'The Aesthetics of Regionalism.' *American Review* 2 (1934): 290–310.

Reyes, Alfonso. 'El paisaje en la poesía mexicana del siglo XIX.' *Obras Completas de Alfonso Reyes*. Vol. 9. Mexico: Fondo de Cultura Economica, 1955. 195. 22 vols.

– 'Visión de Anáhuac.' *Obras Completas de Alfonso Reyes*. Vol. 22. Mexico: Fondo de Cultura Economica, 1955. 99–103. 22 vols.

Reyes, Carmen Sánchez. *Carlos Fuentes y* La región más transparente. Diss. Universidad de Puerto Rico 1973. Puerto Rico: Colleción Uprex, 1975.

Rosenthal, Bernard. *City of Nature: Journeys to Nature in the Age of American Romanticism*. Newark: U of Delaware P, 1980.

Ross, Sinclair. *As for Me and My House*. Toronto: McClelland and Stewart, 1941. Rpt. with intro. by Roy Daniells, 1970.

Ruzicka, William T. *Faulkner's Fictive Architecture: The Meaning of Place in the Yoknapatawpha Novels*. Ann Arbor: U.M.I Research P, 1987.

Salgado, María A. 'El mito Azteca en *La región más transparente*.' *Homenaje a Carlos Fuentes: Variaciones interpretativas en torno a su obra*. Ed. Helmy F. Giacoman. New York: L.A. Publishing, 1971. 229–40.

Sarabia, Rosa. 'Buenos Aires in the 1920s: A Center Within the Margin.' Trans. Laurence de Looze. *Representing Regionalism: New Approaches to the Field*. Ed. David Jordan. New York: Garland, forthcoming.

Séjourné, Laurette. *Burning Water: Thought and Religion in Ancient Mexico*. Trans. Irene Nicholson. New York: Vanguard P, n.d.

Shipley, Joseph T., ed. *Dictionary of World Literature: Criticism, Forms, Technique*. New York: The Philosophical Library, 1943.

Slemon, Stephen. 'Magic Realism as Post-Colonial Discourse.' *Canadian Literature* 116 (Spring 1988): 9–24.

Slotkin, Richard. *The Fatal Environment: The Myth of the Frontier in the Age of Industrialization*. New York: Atheneum, 1985.

Smitten, Jeffrey R. and Ann Daghistany, eds. *Spatial Form in Narrative*. Ithaca and London: Cornell UP, 1981.

Söderlind, Sylvia. *Margin/alia(s): Language and Colonization in Canadian and Québécois Fiction*. Toronto: U of Toronto P, 1991.

Sommers, Joseph. *After the Storm: Landmarks of the Modern Mexican Novel*. Albuquerque: U of New Mexico P, 1968.

Southard, Bruce. 'Syntax and Time in Faulkner's *Go Down, Moses*.' *Language and Style* 14 (Spring 1981): 107–115.

Spanos, William. *Repetitions: The Postmodern Occasion in Literature and Culture*. Baton Rouge and London: Louisiana State UP, 1987.

– 'Modern Literary Criticism and the Spatialization of Time: An Existential Critique.' *Journal of Aesthetics and Art Criticism* 29.1 (Fall, 1970): 87–104.

Stewart, George R. 'The Regional Approach to Literature.' *College English* 9.7 (1948): 370–1.

Suleiman, Susan R. 'The Question of Readability in Avant-Garde Fiction.' *Studies in Twentieth Century Literature* 6. 1–2 (1981–82): 17–35.

Süssekind, Flora. *Tal Brasil, Qual Romance? Uma ideologia estética e sua história: o naturalismo.* Rio de Janeiro: Achiamé, 1984.

Távora, Franklin. *O cabeleira.* 1876. Rio de Janeiro: Edicões Melhoramentos, 1963.

Thoreau, Henry David. 'Walking.' 1843. Rpt. in *The Writings of Henry David Thoreau.* Vol. 5. Boston and New York: Houghton, 1906. 222–3. 11 vols.

Tick, Stanley. 'The Unity of *Go Down, Moses,*' *Twentieth Century Literature* 8 (1962): 69–73.

Tiffin, Helen, 'Commonwealth Literature: Comparison and Judgement.' *The History and Historiography of Commonwealth Literature.* Ed. Dieter Ripmenschneider. Tubingen: Gunter narr, 1983. 30–43.

Verissimo, José. 'Literatura regional.' 1912. Rpt. in *José Veríssimo: Teoria, crítica e história literária.* Ed. João Alexandre Burbosa. São Paulo: Ed. da Universidade dc São Paulo, 1977. 83–7.

Vickery, Olga. *The Novels of William Faulkner.* 1959. Louisiana: Louisiana State UP, 1964.

Wagner, Linda Welshimer, ed. *William Faulkner: Four Decades of Criticism.* Ann Arbor: Michigan State UP, 1973.

Warren, Robert Penn. 'Not Local Color.' *The Virginia Quarterly Review* 1 (1932): 153–60.

– Introduction. *A Southern Harvest.* Boston: Houghton, 1937. xi–xvi.

Watson, Sheila. *The Double Hook.* 1959. Toronto: McClelland and Stewart, 1969.

– 'It's What You Say.' *In Their Words: Interviews With Fourteen Canadian Writers.* Ed. Bruce Meyer and Brian O'Riordan. Toronto: Anansi, 1984. 157–67.

– 'What I'm Going to Do.' *Sheila Watson and* The Double Hook. Ed. George Bowering. Ottawa: The Golden Dog, 1985. 13–15.

Wellek, René. 'The Concept of "Romanticism" in Literary History.' *Comparative Literature* Vol. 1 (1949), 1, 1–23, and Vol. 2, 147–172.

– 'Symbol and Symbolism in Literature.' *Dictionary of the History of Ideas.* Ed. Philip Wiener. Vol 4. New York: Charles Scribner's Sons, 1973. 337–45. 4 vols.

Wells, Walter. *Tycoons and Locusts: A Regional Look at Hollywood Fiction of the 1930s.* Carbondale and Edwardsville: Southern Illinois UP, 1973.

Whitman, Walt. 'The Prairies and Great Plains in Poetry.' 1876. Rpt. in *Walt Whitman: Complete Poetry and Collected Prose.* New York: The Library of America, 1982. 863.

Wilde, Alan. *Middle Grounds: Studies in Contemporary American Fiction.* Philadelphia: U of Pennsylvania P, 1987.

Williams, Frederick G. '*Vidas sêcas* de Graciliano Ramos: Aspectos de una Obra Maestra del Realismo.' *Revista de Cultura Brasileña* 36 (1973): 112–29.

Yáñez, Agustín. *La tierra pródiga*. México: Fondo de Cultura Económica, 1960.

Zola, Emile. 'The Experimental Novel.' 1880. Rpt. in *Documents of Modern Literary Realism*. Ed. and trans. George J. Becker. Princeton, N.J.: Princeton UP, 1963. 161–96.

Index